WOMEN
~ and the ~
GREAT WAR

Bruce Scates

BA (Hons), Dip.Ed., Ph.D.

Raelene Frances

BA (Hons), MA, Ph.D.

To the memory of Janice Mary Anderson, 1958–83, and to 'Sunny Jim'

Peace is the dove who flies
  In the wind and carries the olive branch.
Peace is the kind lamb
  Who grazes on the grass so green.
Peace is the land of Narnia
  Where bravery triumphs over evil.
Bill Scates Frances, aged 9

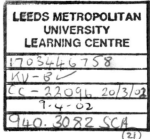

PUBLISHED BY THE PRESS SYNDICATE OF THE UNIVERSITY OF CAMBRIDGE
The Pitt Building, Trumpington Street, Cambridge, United Kingdom

CAMBRIDGE UNIVERSITY PRESS
The Edinburgh Building, Cambridge CB2 2RU, UK http://www.cup.cam.ac.uk
40 West 20th Street, New York, NY 10011–4211, USA http://www.cup.org
10 Stamford Road, Oakleigh, Melbourne 3166, Australia

© Cambridge University Press, 1997

First published 1997

Printed in Australia by Brown Prior Anderson

Typeset in 11/14 Veljovic Book

National Library of Australia Cataloguing in Publication data
Scates, Bruce.
Women and the Great War.
Includes index.
ISBN 0 521 46928 X.
1. Women—Australia—History.
2. World War, 1914–1918—Women.
3. World War, 1914–1918—Australia. I. Frances, Raelene. II. Title.
940.30820994

A catalogue record for this book is available from the British Library
ISBN 0 521 46928 X paperback

Library of Congress Cataloguing in Publication data
CIP data applied for.

CONTENTS

ACKNOWLEDGEMENTS

This book could not have been written without the cooperation, encouragement and financial support of the Australian War Memorial in Canberra. The authors extend their thanks to Ann-Marie Condé, Bobbie Oliver, Peter Stanley and the Memorial's other helpful and generous staff.

Thanks are also due to the many other research centres which provided assistance and material, in particular: the Australian National Library and the Noel Butlin Archives of Business and Labour (Canberra); the Mitchell Library and the State Library of New South Wales (Sydney); the La Trobe Library and State Library of Victoria (Melbourne); the Australian Government Archives (Melbourne); The University of Melbourne Archives; the Victorian Public Records Office (Laverton); the Barr Smith Library (Adelaide); the Battye Library and State Library of Western Australia (Perth); the Oxley Library (Brisbane) and the State Library of Tasmania. We also thank the archivists and staff of the Sydney Girls High School and the staff of the Sydney War Memorial.

The University of New South Wales enabled us to visit the war cemeteries in France and England and the Australian War Graves Commission generously assisted us with information. We also thank Frances Anderson, who cared for our children during our overseas leave. Thanks are also due to Karina Adil, Eddie Scates, Michael and Kathleen Prentice, Ray Anderson, Joanna Sassoon, Shirley Metcalfe, the Wilmot family, and our children Bill and Alex, all of whom assisted us in various ways during this project. Gary Underwood, Cathy Cheng, Jillian Coates, Margot Holden, and the staff of Cambridge University Press showed their usual patience, professionalism and good will.

Editing of source material

In the interests of readability, and mindful that many readers will be secondary school students, the authors have been obliged to 'correct' inconsistencies and errors in the spelling and punctuation of several documents. This intervention is largely confined to extracts from nurses' diaries — often written under very trying conditions. Most source material, however, is reproduced as in the original. We hope this strikes an acceptable balance between the conventions of historical narrative on the one hand and educational purposes on the other.

INTRODUCTION: 'WAR IS WOMEN'S BUSINESS'

1

War is Women's Business

Who face death in order to give life to men? WOMEN.

Who love and work to rear the sons who then are killed in battle? WOMEN.

Who plant fields and harvest crops when all able-bodied men are called to war? WOMEN.

Who keep shops and schools and work in factories while men are in the trenches? WOMEN.

Who nurse the wounded, feed the sick, support the helpless, brave all danger? WOMEN.

Who see their homes destroyed by shell and fire, their little ones made destitute, their daughters outraged? WOMEN.

Who are sent adrift, alone, no food, no hope, no shelter for the unborn child? WOMEN.

Who must suffer agony for every soldier killed? WOMEN.

Who are called upon to make sacrifices to pay the terrible tax of war? WOMEN.

Who dares to say that war is not their business? In the name of Justice and Civilisation give women a voice in Government and in the councils that make or prevent war.
(*Woman Voter*, 21 March 1916)

In 1993, a party of Australian soldiers and civilians gathered at Villers-Bretonneux. Seventy-five years earlier, the site had been the scene of one of the bloodiest battles of the First World War — the Great War. Today it is the final resting place of thousands of Australian soldiers who died there, defending a French village 20 000 kilometres from their home.

For a time the group walked slowly around the cemetery, pausing over the names of men they had never known. One grave was chosen among thousands of others; 'Known only to God' read the inscription on the stone. The remains of this unknown soldier were shaken free of soil, placed in a coffin and draped with an Australian flag. Before the group left, someone scribbled a message in the visitors book: 'We will take care of him now.'

They took him home. On Remembrance Day 1993, the body of Australia's Unknown Soldier was placed in a crypt at the centre of the War Memorial in Canberra. He was buried with full military honours, with pomp and solemn ceremony, with speeches and flowers. A slouch hat rested on the centre of the coffin; it was a powerful symbol of national identity. No one knew the name of this soldier killed a lifetime ago; but he was an Australian — one of our own. The Prime Minister went even further. In a moving address, Paul Keating depicted the Unknown Soldier as a representative not only of the dead of the Great War but of all the conflicts this century, wars in near and distant lands that had claimed 100 000 Australian lives: 'He is *all* of them', Mr Keating declared, 'and he is all of us.'

The entombment of the Unknown Soldier raises a number of important themes. As the Prime Minister himself put it, it was part of the making and remaking of a distinctly Australian legend. The landing of Australian troops at Gallipoli, our first bloody engagement in a long and bloody war, is remembered not as a military defeat, but as a triumph of Australian courage and resourcefulness, a nation's 'baptism of fire'.

For generations, the Anzac legend has been celebrated in our history books; it is part of our national folklore, part of our sense of ourselves. But as the Prime Minister's speech also suggested, this legend, like all other legends, rested on a number of exclusions. It was a legend which excluded those who had not gone to war; and it was a legend made exclusively by men. A nation had found its identity not in peace but in war, in destruction and chaos, in fear, pain and death. It is something of an irony that men are seen as giving 'birth' to a nation and that the birth of a nation is found in the death of its youth.

Legends aside, the reality is that the soldier buried in Canberra can never represent Australia's experience of the Great War. War, as our opening poem suggests, is not just soldiers' business; it alters and claims the lives of women as well as men. Our memory of that conflict is alarmingly incomplete. We remember the men who fought and fell in battle but not the sacrifice of those who nursed the dying and wounded; we celebrate the achievement of armies but not those who toiled to feed and clothe them; we pay tribute to the remains of unknown soldiers but know surprisingly little about the pain of bereavement and loss. And we know little of these things because they are essentially women's experience of war: the experience of nurses not soldiers; of the home front, not the battlefield; of those who knew the grief, not the 'glory', of war.

If war is not simply men's business, it isn't *simply* women's either. Women's (and men's) experience of war is varied and diverse. This book explores differences and conflicts among women: between the women who supported the war and those who opposed it; between those who suffered the loss of husbands, sons and fathers and those who did not. It also identifies groups of women who contested or threatened the so-called national interest: women of German descent and women whose sexual or political behaviour undermined the war effort in a number of different ways.

This book is an attempt to retrieve women's experience from the carnage and the myth making of the Great War. It relies on the voices of the women themselves. From private and public testimonies, letters, diaries, contemporary books, journals and newspapers, and a host of historical studies, we have tried to glean different versions of our past. And we have reproduced these voices in many documents and illustrations so that students of history might listen and judge for themselves.

Figure 1.1

The burden of war
(Mitchell Library, Ref. GPO 1
Frame 23180)

■ This sculpture, 'Sacrifice', dominates the War Memorial in Sydney. What point is it making?

WORK IN THE BATTLE ZONES: NURSING THE TROOPS

2

Figure 2.1

NSW nurses embarking for France
(*Punch*, 13 July 1916)

■ How old do these women appear to be?

Anzac Day is the public holiday which probably means most to the majority of Australians. For generations, old and young have gathered together in the grey light of dawn, stood in silence and remembered. Even 80 years after the Anzac landing, the services have lost none of their sorrow, none of their solemnity. The parades which take place on Anzac Day and the response of the thousands of spectators tell us a great deal about the way in which Australians remember the wars in which we have fought. At the 1995 Sydney parade, for instance, a boy was seen enthusiastically waving a placard which read: 'Good on you boys!' Yet, in the lines which marched past him were hundreds of women war veterans. Most prominent of these were the women from the Australian Army Nursing Service, which has a distinguished history of service in combat zones dating back to that first fateful landing at Gallipoli.

The 2500 nurses who served during the Great War have been largely forgotten by Australians. We have focused our attention on

the heroic figure of the digger, arguably one of the most compelling symbols of our national identity. This is understandable; men were far more likely to die at war than women; men paid the heavy price of victory. But that does not change the fact that women also worked and suffered for their country in wartime; many died in the same cause and lie buried among their menfolk. The experiences of these Australian women at war form the focus of this chapter.

Enlisting

When war was declared in August 1914, Australians generally greeted the news with great excitement and enthusiasm. Men and women alike rushed to offer their services for the war effort. Nurses were particularly keen to join up, seeing an obvious need for their skills in the inevitable conflict. This would not necessarily be their first experience of military nursing. Some had already served their country in the so-called Boer War of 1898–1902, when each of the colonies had sent military contingents to help the British Government defeat the Afrikaners in South Africa. Many of the nurses who had volunteered for service in South Africa (many paying their own fares) did so out of a desire to improve the status of the nursing profession in general. The English nurse, Florence Nightingale, had started this process some 40 years earlier during the Crimean War. Her ideals of professional, ladylike nursing practice, with its scrupulous attention to order and cleanliness, were being introduced in Australia in the 1880s and 1890s.

The nurses who went to South Africa hoped that serving their country would further improve the reputation of nursing as a respectable occupation for well-brought-up young ladies. They were not disappointed. The British military authorities were originally reluctant to employ female nurses, as they believed them unsuited to the demands of military nursing. Eventually, however, these prejudices were overcome and after the war it was accepted that women would perform an important part in future medical care of troops.

In 1902, soon after the six colonies had joined to form the Commonwealth of Australia, the Australian Army Nursing Service was formed. The first nurses left for active service within months of the declaration of war and their numbers would be added to with each ship leaving for the theatre of war.

Who were these women and why were they so keen to go to war? To join the Army, nurses had to be aged between 21 and 40 years. Most were at least 24 since in those days nurses did not usually begin training until they were 20 or 21. Some worked for the Red Cross and others found their own way to Europe and worked in British or French hospitals.

Nurses generally shared a common class background. Trainees needed to have some source of income other than the tiny wages they received — a factor which made it very difficult for working-class women to undertake the three-year course. By the early twentieth century, nurses tended to come from middle-class families, often with fathers in the professions or business, or in farming. It was fortunate that most of these women came from relatively well-off families, since going to war involved them in a lot of personal expense. In some states they were given donations to help with these expenses but in others they had to find the money themselves. A Victorian nurse, Sister Evelyn Davies, complained about the lack of proper provisioning: 'Look at...how much it cost [us] in Australia, then since coming to London [we] have had to buy Primus Stoves, Mackintoshes, Gum Boots, Mess kit and several odds and ends.'[1] The Army provided none of these items.

For most nurses, the motives in volunteering were no doubt mixed. Many felt it was their patriotic duty to do what they could to help their country and, perhaps more importantly, the Empire, in its hour of need. The war also offered opportunities which they would not have at home to gain valuable professional experience which would advance their careers when peace returned. And like so many of the soldiers, they were seized by a sense of adventure at the prospect of visiting new places and gaining new personal experiences. Sister Evelyn 'Tevie' Davies welcomed every opportunity for new experiences, the more remote and strange the location the better. As she wrote to her mother after volunteering to go to India, 'I wouldn't have an opportunity of living in India perhaps ever again it will be an experience quite apart from what we have before had.'[2] She felt sorry for her mother left behind with 'always the same dull round' while she was 'always experiencing something new'. And for a good many, romance and adventure were inextricable. 'Half the women here are keen on getting married', Tevie told her mother, adding that 'it is to be hoped there are men enough left for them.'[3]

For some nurses a major motive was their desire to be with loved ones who were leaving with the expeditionary force. Many of the nurses had brothers and sweethearts serving with the AIF (Australian Imperial Force) and some, like Sister Elsie Cook, were married — although, officially, sisters were supposed to be single. Elsie Sheppard had married Syd, the son of the former Prime Minister Joseph Cook, shortly before he left for the war. She followed a few months later. Four years later, with the war still going on, she recalled the high spirits and hopes they had had during their brief honeymoon: together they would 'do their bit' for the Empire.[4]

Document 2.1

A nurse's views on women

It has been argued that the war nurses were true pioneers in the cause of women, breaking down barriers to women's employment in the hitherto 'male' military sphere. Their diaries and letters give us some clues as to their views on women's role in society.

London, 15 July 1915

I have sent a paper Mum dear of the Women's procession yesterday. It was very long but still I don't see the sense of it much but the Suffragettes simply must keep before the public. Anyhow it's better than smashing windows etc. Still a woman's place is in her own home first I consider.

On board ship from Egypt to Bombay, 22 March 1916

...Mrs Daniels who had been Matron at the Hostel was being given a send-off this night. She came on the stage dressed as a Sister minus the red cape and sang rather well [and] the boys applauded loudly. After a pause she came back gently mopping her eyes; however, she valiantly sang a bar of 'The Lost Chord' then with further patting of her eyes she said in a tragic voice, 'It's no use boys, I can't sing tonight' (a kind of a ring-down-the-curtain act). The boys thought it most pathetic, but of course the Nurses thought it most affected, being unsentimental beings. At the close of the entertainment she was presented with a basket of flowers. She again wept, thereby gaining further applause. I think I'll have to adopt these feminine traits. Maybe I shall go off this season then [become engaged during the next social season].

Peshawar, India, 24 November 1916

We had an argument at the Mess recently. The head Sister said that women were practically the root of all evil, she didn't know what the world was coming to, that they were not dependable [and] she preferred a man for they [sic] were true. I flared up and asked her what about her own Mother? She caved in and said that nowadays the women were different. The fact of the matter [is that] she strives to keep up with officers' wives who do nothing but entertain Subalterns and lead gay lives. She finds they look down on a nursing Sister, then gets piqued with women in general. They make me tired.

(Letters of Sister Evelyn Davies [to her mother], 3DRL 3398, Australian War Memorial)

■ How would you describe Evelyn Davies' views on women?

Off to the war

Embarking for service overseas stirred a curious mixture of emotions. In the final hours before boarding the troopships, nurses spoke of their sadness at leaving home and loved ones, and of their wonder and apprehension at the great adventure before them. Whatever the feelings, the last few days in Australia were a flurry of activity: scribbling letters to friends and family, squeezing into ill-fitting uniforms and 'the awful shuffle' of cramming kit and belongings into a few cases.

On board ship, the pace of activity slowed considerably. It was a long journey. Nurses bound for England from eastern Australia called briefly at the port of Fremantle, then sailed to Cape Town and up the west coast of Africa to Britain. Others took the Suez route to Egypt, or travelled by ship and then by train and cart through the vast expanse of India. Women, who may never have left home before, left Australia 20 000 kilometres behind them.

Document 2.2

Leaving for the war

(Letters of Sister Evelyn Davies, 3DRL 3398B, Australian War Memorial)

> Barrington Avenue
> East Kew
> 17-5-'15.
>
> My Dear Mummie
> I tried so hard to come home again tonight but couldnt manage it I was dreadfully sorry too for I fully made up my mind to come anyhow perhaps it was as well we would only have had the parting all over again. Mum Dear I know you will be feeling terribly lonely, but dont worry Dear I'll soon be home again. Poor Mum you have always been the unselfish one, I'll always be thinking of you, and wishing I could help you to bed again. How I'll long for you all and the dear old mountains Goodness only knows, and Stumpy too never mind Mum I'll never alter, and will still help you milk when I come home I got my uniform today, and will have to wear it tomorrow, it is not at all elegant however looks are not everything I got the luggage away alright although it was an awful scuffle at the last I got the Cheque from the Department alright, and settled up the accounts so tomorrow will be clear I just dread thinking of going, but it will be alright once I get away. Good bye My Own Mummie Dear Don't fret you know the others are near Rupe is Son & daughter too far better than I have been Cheer up Mum Darling I'll write soon

■ This letter was written by Evelyn Davies to her mother just before embarkation. What emotions does it reveal and what does it tell us about Evelyn's social background and domestic responsibilities?

The months spent at sea often passed slowly. Sea sickness was a common complaint, particularly on that first rough crossing around the Bight to Fremantle. And on some ships nurses had to contend with even more serious illness. An outbreak of disease on one transport ship killed many soldiers; others were coaxed back to health by sick, exhausted nurses. It was on board ship that nurses had their first taste of Army regulations.

So far as military etiquette was concerned, nurses were officers and not permitted to associate with the soldiers who travelled on the decks below them. If weather allowed they could promenade the length of the ship but after 9.30 p.m. they were confined

Document 2.3

A visit to Perth

At Subiaco, the streets are all well planted with Pepper Trees and Moreton Bay Figs. We went through beautiful country to Nedlands. It seems strange to us after Melbourne to have trams moving right through the bush. Such glorious colouring — the bush with its orange-coloured flowers and the flowering gum at its best. At Nedlands, we did full justice to a cup of tea with hot scones and cake. It is surprising how hungry one gets. The river here widens like a bay and there are many yachts and fishing boats on it. The men repairing the fishing nets, the children paddling at the water's edge and the beautiful gardens all…helped to make a charming picture.

(Diary of Sister Elsie Tranter, 11 January 1916, DRL 4081, Australian War Memorial)

■ Almost all the outward-bound nurses called in at Fremantle. For others, the bluff at Albany would be their last glimpse of Australia. In her account of her brief stay in Perth, why does Elsie Tranter describe the people and the landscape so fondly?

to their cabins. Writing, reading, sewing, coits and other deck games, filled up most of the day but many nurses longed to know 'the boys' a little better. Sister Elsie Tranter and her friends spent many a morning watching the men exercising; the evening church services were even more exciting: 'the boys and the nurses all grouped round the Padre singing…the moon making paths of gold across the water'.[5] By their seventh week at sea, they had 'set up a lively correspondence with the decks below', several of the ship's officers 'acting as their postman'.[6] And secretive letters led to even more secretive meetings:

We did not get much sleep last night… Peg came with us after dinner and I tried to steal a few minutes conversation with one of the 'Forbidden Diggers'. The sentry was bored enough to keep watch for us and he said to Peg, 'Love-makin' on the Ship is like mashin' a girl with her father watching. You've got to be up to all sorts of tricks.'[7]

■ What do Elsie Tranter's Ten Commandments tell us about the relationship between **(a)** the nurses and the SMOs, and **(b)** the nurses and the troops?
■ What does she mean by 'thou…must be kept sacred'?

Document 2.4

Ten Commandments for Sisters

1 The S.M.O. [Senior Medical Officer] is our only God. Thou shalt have no one but him.
2 Thou shalt not make graven images of the S.M.O. and officers that fly in the Heavens above [and]…think they own this boat.
3 Sisters, thou shalt not take the name of the S.M.O. in vain — when he punishes thee for being out of bounds after dark and gives thee three nights' hard labour on duty.
4 Six days shalt thou talk to thyself and on the seventh keep thy mouth shut.
5 Honour thy Steward[s]…for they only are essential to thy happiness.
6 Thou shalt kill rats and other vermin but leave the captain and Major…still alive.
7 Thou shalt not adulterate thy nurse's life with joy…
8 Thou shalt not steal kisses in the dark, cosy corners on the deck or in covered areas. At any rate, do not be found out.
9 Thou shalt not bear false witness against the lady passengers.
10 Thou shalt not covet thee civilian cabins, nor clothes, nor liberties, nor drinks, nor any other things that do not belong to thee — nor officers from other boats for thou art on active service and thou…must be kept sacred.

(Tranter Diary, 18 January 1917, 3DRL 4081, Australian War Memorial)

It is difficult to establish what the sentry really meant by 'love-makin'. For most nurses, meetings with the troops were confined to harmless flirtation; and while Elsie Tranter enjoyed the rough and ready company of the men, many young ladies preferred the polite conversation of the officers. On the other hand, a good many of the nurses who served abroad found husbands among their charges, some marrying men well 'beneath' their social station. Several were actually returned home for 'misbehaviour'; the authorities were determined to prevent such sexual liaisons.

Romance was not the only distraction on the journey out from Australia. A voyage across the oceans opened a city girl's eyes to the wonders of nature; diaries record 'the effect of sun upon the spray', 'the golden sunsets' and the moon 'rising like a ball of fire from the water'. And as the ships drew into port, Australian nurses prepared themselves for their first encounter with new lands, new peoples and new cultures. Letters home abound with descriptions of 'this Great Eastern Land' (Egypt); wide-eyed with wonder they strolled through the ruins of antiquity, fought their way through the bustle of the markets and gazed upon a landscape altogether new to them. Alice Kitchen scribbled excitedly in her diary:

Figure 2.2
Enthusiastic tourists: Australian Army Nursing Service sisters, on their first tour of duty in 1915
(AWM AO5410)

■ Why were such excursions so popular with nursing staff?

This afternoon I went for a walk round the pyramid. [I went] down to the Sphinx and stood looking at it for some time, surrounded by soldiers, Arabs, camels and donkeys. The soldiers were out to enjoy the day having camel and donkey rides, climbing the pyramid & even under the chin of the Sphinx. I saw one climbing & cutting his name on one of the stones of the pyramid. It was all a glorious picture.[8]

The people proved equally exotic. Australia's nurses came from a largely white and culturally homogenous society. Few had met Aboriginal people or heard a language other than English. Now they were surrounded by 'crowds of little coolies and Kaffir children' begging, singing and dancing for their pennies. Often the children are described as 'lovely'; the 'bright coloured clothes', bracelets and earrings seemed picturesque and beguiling. The spectacle of 'coloured' men at work provoked an uglier sort of racism. Elsie Tranter reported in her diary:

Towards evening the coal bunkers came alongside. Fortunately the nigs [sic] on these bunkers wear a few clothes, bright coloured pants and all manner of strange garments. They are more like animals than human beings and have reduced the art of loafing and panting to the finest. Any excuse is sufficient to make them stop work… We throw down pennies…cigarettes and scraps of food. Down go the baskets all at once [and they] fight for [these trifles]… We have no shore leave the country being so unhealthy but we get amusement enough watching the nigs.[9]

Ultimately the joke was at Elsie's own expense. Like most Australian nurses, she had left her country hoping to broaden her mind; instead this meeting with a new culture strengthened older fears and prejudices.

The shopping, sightseeing and sexual adventure soon came to an end. Within a few months of leaving home, the carefree diversions of the tourist gave way to the terrible realities of war.

Figure 2.3

Sisters of 3rd Australian General Hospital at Abbassia lining up for a donkey race
(AWM JO1748)

■ What do you think the military authorities would have thought about this behaviour?

■ Elsie Tranter confined her racism to a few remarks in her letters and her diary. The men's response was often more violent. How does Sister Richmond see the behaviour of her countrymen?

Document 2.5

A nurse's response to the Cairo riots

1.4.15: Good Friday. Went to morning service. This evening there was a riot in town, the New Zealanders and Australians being well in it. The real cause lay between a Maori and [a] native woman so New Zealanders and our men joined in. The things were taken out of many shops and set fire to. The Territorials [British troops stationed in Egypt] were called in to keep order. Shots were fired and a great many injured.

2.4.15: We hear to-day all Australians and many New Zealanders are being sent away as the result of this. Even tonight there was another riot at Heliopolis at some picture show. What makes all these men behave like this, so disgracing all our land and people? The Territorials are holding themselves as so superior and up here one hears very one-sided accounts.

(Diary of Sister Daisy Richmond, 2DRL 783, Australian War Memorial)

Gallipoli

Australia's first real experience of war was on the steep and unforgiving slopes of the Gallipoli Peninsula. The Allies had expected an easy victory and landed the 'untried' Australian and New Zealand troops on what they believed were poorly defended beaches. Instead, the Anzacs stumbled from their landing craft into a blaze of Turkish machine guns; on the first day alone 500 were killed and several thousand wounded. British and other allied casualties were even higher. Confident of a quick campaign, the Allied command had made little provision for the wounded.

Figure 2.4

Staff Nurse Clarice Daley weds Sergeant Ernie Lawrence of the Australian Light Horse in a tent on Lemnos, c. September 1915.
(AWM P1360/02/01)

■ Why did the military authorities discourage such liaisons?

For many hours they lay exposed upon the narrow beaches, showered by enemy gunfire. Those who survived were laid out on transports and slowly towed away to safety. The nurses waited to receive them, stationed on hospital ships off shore or in the hospital camps of Lemnos and Alexandria.

Work on the hospital ships was probably the most trying. Expecting light casualties, the ships catered for a few hundred patients; within hours of the landing the decks were cluttered with several thousand wounded. Sister Lydia King was stationed on the S.S. *Sicilia*, moored off Cape Helles. She was one of the few women to witness the Gallipoli landing:

I shall never forget the awful feeling of hopelessness. On night duty it was dreadful. I had two wards downstairs and over a 100 patients, and then I had a small ward upstairs and some officers, altogether about 250 patients to look after with one orderly [to help me].[10]

By August, there were six hospital ships anchored off the cove. As young Australians were ordered to their slaughter at the Nek and Lone Pine, these ships filled with their 'cargo of human suffering'. Alice Kitchen was stationed on the *Gascon*. The game boys she had watched climbing the pyramids a few months earlier died 'dirty and dry and hungry':

A busy day as usual…[another batch of wounded] one abdominal among them; quite a huge wound and awful gore everywhere; two other abdominals in, dying. They seem so hopeless…a bad haemorrhage leg came in also which looks ominous… [Thirty more] stretchers came in at 9.30 pm…we had to put them on the hatchway. We stayed with a dying man making the third that day…up till late at night trying to straighten things out a little.[11]

At the base hospitals in Egypt conditions were not much better. On the morning of 30 April, Elsie Cook went on duty 'in an empty ward', a hastily converted boys school. Within 24 hours 'everything looked disorder and chaos'. Her diary entry reflects this:

On entering the ward, — boots, packs, bandages, blood stained tunics, etc greeted the eye, everywhere…the poor old patients looked miserable & dirty & as if they hadn't slept a wink. — Terribly short staff in the hospital, — we have got 700 badly wounded men and six Sisters & Matron! — wounded still arriving in hundreds, tents being put up in the grounds to make extra room…dressing from early morning till late at night, without a stop.[12]

The operating theatres worked all through the night, amputating limbs and digging out shot and shrapnel. Many of the wounds, Sister Cook noted, 'had not been touched for days'; men died of gangrene and infection more than their actual injuries. Amid the cries of dying men, she received news that her husband Syd had been wounded. In every shattered face, she must have imagined his agony.

Gallipoli has often been seen as Australia's 'baptism of fire'. Despite the tragic waste of life, the bravery of the Anzacs is thought to have overshadowed the suffering. The nurses who dealt with the casualties of war had a very different perception of the landing. To them, this 'dreadful war' was nothing but 'wholesale murder'.[13] After four days of broken sleep and endless work, Sister Lydia King scrawled a bitter message in her diary:

One loses sight of all the honour & glory in work such as we are dealing with. We have nought but the horrors the primary results of the War. Nothing will induce any of our Staff to tell of the horrors they have seen & dealt with & no one who has not seen it in its awful reality could imagine a portion of this saddest part of the war.[14]

In the end, it was not just the battles which claimed men's lives. Young Australians died (as we've seen) because British commanders had taken so little care in planning the landing. In a way, those first terrible days set the pattern of the entire campaign: from beginning to end, Gallipoli was a tragic fiasco. And no one was more conscious of this criminal incompetence than the nurses. Forty miles from the firing line, Matron Wilson wrote a confused and angry letter to her sister:

Things seems so badly organised — of course I know it is an appalling business to cope with — still some people can't organise — we were three weeks in London always packed and ready to leave at an hour's notice — then a transport or rather four transports — because we were all split up on to different boats — brought us to Alexandria — The Officers and men came on here a week ago — to find *nothing*, the boat with their equipment no one has heard of — and here they are all lying on the stones with the sky above them — medical men well known in Australia — such as Col Fiaschi — Sir Alex. McCormick, Professor Martin and many others who have given up from 3 to 5 and even 8 thousand a year to come. Not even a tent can they beg or steal. We arrived (after being in a hotel in Alexandria until Monday) yesterday — on a hospital ship — and of course it is no use going ashore — we are living on the boat in the meantime in the harbour — and when the ship goes to pick up wounded, we will have to transfer to another if the tents have not arrived. If only they had allowed the colonel to bring everything on one ship — would be alright — but they would not allow it — bits of everything come on every ship — nothing is complete — they all arrive useless…if you can imagine…a bare piece of ground, covered with stones — the size of from pebbles to boulders — the men and officers in their clothes lying on it, food, army rations being drawn each day from the army service, and we sisters imprisoned on a ship, opposite, doing nothing — you have No. 3. Aust. Gen. Hosp.[15]

Matron Wilson had far more than the responsibilities of her job to cope with. She worried constantly about her two soldier brothers, one of whom had gone missing on the Peninsula a few days before she wrote the above letter. Her dearest hope, like that of other nurses who knew what war wounds could mean, was that he was killed quickly. (In fact, he was shot by a sniper at Quinn's Post and bled to death before help could reach him.) The physical stress of working long hours in appalling conditions was made so much worse by such anxiety over relatives and friends on the battlefield and in the hospitals.

The physical suffering of the campaign was not confined to the soldiers. Nurses and men alike lived in flimsy makeshift shelters; in winter they were freezing, in summer they worked 'in a bath of perspiration'. Water was short and the rations often rancid, men and women alike broke their teeth on tasteless Army biscuits. And nurses, like their patients, came under fire when the ships went in to pick up wounded. Sister Richmond's diary entry for 11 August 1915 gives some idea of the danger:

We return to Imbros [and] discharge our light cases [the not so badly wounded, and] once more return to be refilled. The girls on day duty are working till 1 and 2 am. as they did the night before. We were well under fire many bullets coming on the decks. I was speaking to one boy [and had] moved away to another patient when a bullet hit him and lodged in the thigh. I just missed it.[16]

After eight months of fruitless fighting, even the most obstinate of the Allied command conceded that the campaign was a failure. It had cost the lives of 30 000 Allied troops, 8000 of whom were Australians. Perhaps as many as 75 000 Turks died defending their homeland. The cost to Australia's nursing staff is more difficult to measure; while none of the nurses who served near Gallipoli was killed in battle, several died of illness and pneumonia. Most were shipped on to England sick and exhausted. And for all of them this 'dreadful war' was only just beginning.

The Western Front

By the time Australian troops reached the Western Front, the war was completely bogged down. The Germans and the Allies had dug into two opposing lines of trenches separated by about 40 metres of 'no-man's-land'. Across a landscape marred with shell holes, wire and wreckage, each side shot at the other. There was no way out of this impasse. With suicidal determination, the Allied Command ordered one 'charge' after another, convinced that men could break through the twisted wire and machine-gun fire and capture the enemy trenches. For almost five years, the Front moved only a few kilometres one way or the other; no-man's-land became the killing fields of Europe. The nurses were caught up in the rhythm of this type of warfare — periods of relative safety and boredom interspersed with 'pushes' during which thousands of men could be mown down in a single day. When a push was on, ambulances streamed into the medical units, or casualty clearing stations, just behind the lines; at other times the wards stood idle, waiting for the next attack and the convoys of wounded and dying men.

The medical staff were more fortunate than the regular soldiers in that they had more things to occupy their time during the lulls between these terrible battles. In 1917 Sister Cook was working for the French Army near Amiens. Her diary lists a busy schedule of social engagements and sight seeing.

12.6.17: Boating on the river, — Fraser and I try to learn to canoe.

13.6.17: Hospital almost empty. General Smith called in his nice car & took Fraser & me out to Bgde Hdqtrs, — where horses were ready & we went for a ride thro' beautiful old 'bais' & across fields. Colonel Somerville came with us. We rode about 10 miles in the Sente direction. Returned home for tennis, played till 8.30 pm, had dinner & drove home.

17.6.17: After coming off duty, we walked out into the country for cornflowers & poppies, brought home armfuls.

18.6.17: Went for a motor drive.

19.6.17: Tubby FitzHill wounded. wrote to Syd.

20.6.17: Went to dinner with Tebbutt and Joe at the Hotel du Rhin.

23.6.17: The French girls & Fraser & I gave a tea party in the hospital garden, Joe Metcalfe, Jose, Fay, Pye & Wheeler came.

24.6.17: Went out to 14th F. Amb. to Urailoy to tennis & mess, met General Hophkink, brigadier of the 14th Bgde.[17]

As the daughter-in-law of a prominent Australian politician, Elsie Cook moved with ease through the highest echelons of the military. But her experience was not exceptional. Even nurses from less distinguished social backgrounds were sought after by the officers; and of course it was only the officers who had access to the tennis courts, expensive restaurants and cars. For all the nurses, even those working very close to the front line, there were avenues of escape, time off duty to stroll through the French countryside and try to forget the ravages of war.

Being in France also meant that soldiers and nurses alike could spend their leave in Britain, or Blighty as many called it. Although eight out of ten of the Army nurses had been born in Australia, England was still regarded as a second home. This was not surprising, since many had parents or grandparents born in the 'old country'. The war provided nurses with a chance to meet up with relatives and to visit the places of their parents' youth. Sister Lydia King, for instance, records a visit to her uncle in Bristol: 'Bonzer Breakfast in bed. Grace, Olive & I drove round first saw Father's old home where he was born also where my parents lived after they were married. I took quite a number of snaps.'[18]

Elsie Cook spent many of her leaves in England where she often managed to meet her husband, an officer with the AIF who had been wounded twice at Gallipoli. On one occasion they spent an idyllic six days cycling around the south-west counties before Syd had to return to his unit. And even those nurses who travelled alone were enchanted by their first experience of Britain; letters to friends and relatives describe the soft beauty of its countryside and the grandeur of its ancient buildings. Of course a leave in Britain was not without its problems. Cities like London felt the effects of the war; there were difficulties in finding transport and accommodation, and even the civilian population feared bombing raids by German zeppelins. Often the best planned leaves were laid to waste. Another of Elsie's diary entries shows just how difficult it was to organise meetings with loved ones in wartime:

6.12.16: Great excitement, — got a telegram from Syd to say he had leave 11–14th & would meet me at Southampton. — Rushed off, & got permission to go to England — & passes, etc, — was given 20 days leave.

11.12.16: [Southampton – Dolphin Hotel] This afternoon a wire from Syd to say he will arrive tonight at 9 pm. Quite excited. Ordered fire in our room & at 9 pm Syd arrived. Spent a very happy evening by the fire.

12.12.16: After lunch a terrible blow fell in the shape of a wire for Syd recalling him to Camp & to leave tonight for France! Packing up & spent an hour waiting for the train, sitting by the fire. Caught a train to Salisbury & went to Camp, helped Syd to pack up & at 8 pm, he left Camp to march down to the Stn, — I, with Will Stewart, motored alongside the column to the Stn. There I watched Syd & his boys entrain for Folkestone, — & go.. Poor old Syd, — another Goodbye.[19]

For the most part, Australian nurses loved England; they were much more divided about the English. Waging war on Germany, it seems, brought out the best and the worst of what the nurses called the 'character' of the English. Elsie Tranter praised the efforts of the women: 'little girls' in London could be seen driving buses and vans through the streets of a busy city, they worked in factories, schools and offices, often performing tasks usually reserved for men. It was a 'good show' she wrote, 'and we were all very grateful'.[20] But other nurses tired of the reserved English character and longed for the frank and open honesty of fellow colonials. By the time of her second leave in London, 'Tevie' Davies had reached the point of exasperation:

Mum, you have no idea what a cramped country it is. I long for space, freedom and Nature in its wild state, not make-believe like the woods are here…if only man hadn't a hand in everything, the people then would be broader minded and less pompous.[21]

Figure 2.5
3rd Australian General Hospital, Cairo, c. 1916
(AWM JO1714)

■ Mascots reinforced a sense of Australianness abroad. What other mementos of home might nurses have taken with them?

The First World War is thought to have shaped a distinctive Australian identity: on the killing fields of Gallipoli and France, young Australian diggers realised the cost of being tied to Britain. It is important to remember that this quest for a sense of ourselves as a separate people was not just a male experience. Australian women who served abroad also realised that being Australian made them different, that England was not the 'Home' they were taught it would be. The Great War was a time of growing up for all Australians.

Active service in France

Leave in England ended soon enough and the nurses were ordered to return to duty. It was a rude awakening. With just a few hours' notice nurses were obliged to pack their gear (no easy task when it included stove, bath, bed and luggage) and organise its transport. They were crammed onto troopships and trains which usually had few amenities for women. When Australian General One Hospital was transferred to Rouen, nurses were forced to stand for several hours, pressed up against a doorway. No toilets were provided for women so they made do with biscuit tins, washing with eau de cologne afterwards.

The journeys were often very dangerous. Troop transports were obvious enemy targets and several nurses lost their lives in actions against them. Elsie Tranter attended the funeral of a Sister Dawson: 'Her body was washed up near our camp', she noted in her diary. 'She was on a hospital ship torpedoed in the channel.' Dawson's remains were laid to rest in a tiny cemetery in France, the coffin 'covered with the union jack and flowers' and three

Figure 2.6

Yet another transfer: nursing staff of 2nd Australian General Hospital, Cairo, waiting to leave for France (AWM PO156/81/43)

■ What were these women likely to be carrying?

Document 2.6

A cold crossing

Such a day. We were all up in good time to commence the last stage of our pilgrimage to France. We were held responsible for all our luggage and had to check it all downstairs before breakfast. Then we got it weighed and registered…and just managed to be pushed into the train as it was leaving… Peg's kitbag and mine were left behind. At Flagstone, we went straight from the train to the boat. There were 76 sisters on. Oh! the cold! The 'Onward' brought us to Bologne… We had to wear our lifebelts all the time so we could not snuggle up together. It took about 1¼ hours to cross the channel. It was pm when we landed and very cold and dark. The first sound from French shores that greeted us was a group of our own soldiers singing 'Keep the Home Fires Burning'. We would have been overjoyed at that moment to have any old fire burning.

(Tranter Diary, 28 February 1917, 3DRL 4081, Australian War Memorial)

■ What were the discomforts and hazards of Elsie's journey?
■ How do you think she felt when she heard Australian singing?

Scottish soldiers playing the bagpipes. As the 'Last Post' was sounded, Elsie must have known that the body in the coffin could well have been any one of them.[22]

The physical discomforts and immediate danger of active service were taxing enough, but what nurses noticed most after having leave was the loss of their individuality. Suddenly their personal life was over and they were back in the Army. Elsie Tranter again: 'It is a rotten day after 14 days of freedom to have to obey the voice of authority. "Stand over there till I am ready!" I felt like a bit of luggage left in the cloak room.'[23]

On the Western Front, memories of a leave in London faded all too quickly. Several of the nurses who served in France and Belgium had seen the effects of war before; the shock of Gallipoli helped to prepare them for the carnage that followed. But most were staring for the first time into the face of such suffering. Unable and often unwilling to write to friends and family about it, a nurse had only her diary in which to record her sorrow:

The road between the hospital and our quarters is the road used by the military and there is a continual tramp of Khaki boys all day… Can you form any idea of the suffering that goes on…in all those lines? It makes one's heart ache to see the ways the dear old boys have suffered and are suffering… With our boys it is not only the wounds — so many of the poor boys are frightfully sick…[and they] are tired out when they come to us.[24]

The boys were lucky to reach the hospitals at all. Although the front line was only a few miles from the casualty clearing stations, roads leading to and from the battlefield were often impassable. The motor ambulances bogged down miles from the Front and the wounded were carried on stretchers or dragged themselves to safety. For days on end men were stranded in no-man's-land; they drowned in mud and flooded shell holes, bled to death, or died of exposure within just a few hundred metres of safety.

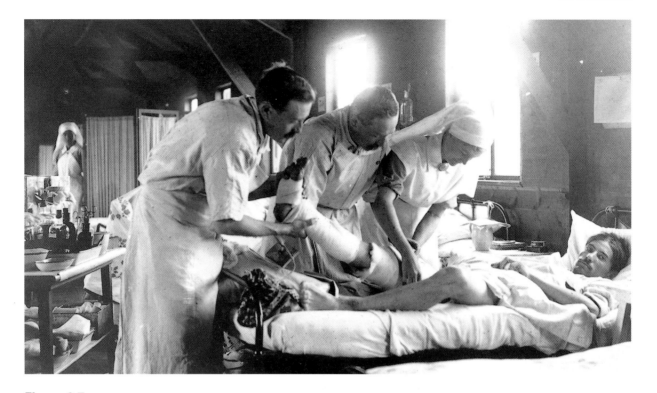

Figure 2.7

Hospital ward, Forges-les-Eaux, France: Sister Lynette Crozier and two medical staff apply dressing to wounded French soldier
(AWM PO1790.001)

■ This picture is obviously staged for the camera. How would this scene have differed from that in a casualty clearing station during a 'push'?

At Gallipoli, the Allies had been caught unprepared for the number of wounded. On the Western Front, where clearing stations littered the line and a string of base hospitals was established behind them, medical staff were still unable to stem the tide of human suffering. Every new push or enemy attack left the wards overflowing with dead, dying and wounded men. And conditions for the nurses had improved little since their time on Lemnos. The best postings were away from the main line — in the hotels, schools and sanatoriums that were converted into hospitals. The casualty clearing stations were much more primitive. Sister Valerie Woinarski described the British station at Vimy Ridge as a simple 'tin shed, erected, camouflaged, and furnished with wooden trestles... Upon [these we] placed stretchers of wounded men awaiting surgical treatment'.[25] But even the largest of camps and hospitals were hastily relocated, nurses and wounded alike fearing capture by the Germans. By March 1918, Elsie Tranter had left the seaside hospital at Etaples for a casualty clearing station near the village of Grevillers. As the enemy advanced on Amiens, she described the suffering and chaos around her:

22.3.18: Such a noisy night. Barrage commenced at 1.5 a.m. Shells were whistling and screaming. We were watching the shrapnel bursting in the air. At 3 a.m. there was a terrific explosion and everything was lighted up. The dump at Baupaume was struck. We three Australians were wondering what would happen next — everything seemed so unreal. When we got over to the Mess we found that most of the staff had been spending the night in the dugout. By 7 a.m. the wounded were pouring in, some in ambulances, some walking, helping one another along.

All day long we worked under very trying conditions. We had four operating tables in constant use and poor fellows lying on stretchers on the theatre floor, waiting till we could attend to them.

One poor chap with half his jaw blown away <u>walked</u> in supported by two wounded comrades.

I gave twenty anaesthetics finishing at 2.30 this morning. Then orders came for us to evacuate and we had hurriedly to make what preparations we could. The wounded were sent by road transport to various Stationary and Base hospitals. We were only allowed such luggage as we could carry so we put on our warmest clothing and filled our coat pockets to overflowing. That waiting time after the wounded had been sent on always will leave two pictures in my memory. The first of the sitting room we had thought so pretty and cosy only a few days before now dismantled and with Sisters all weary and sleepy — some sitting about, some lying on the floor with a gas mask for a pillow trying to snatch a few minutes sleep; the other of the same party of Sisters sitting on the roadside waiting for transport, tin hats on at various and unbecoming angles, pockets bulging and all wondering 'What next?'[26]

Two days later Elsie found herself in the church of a nearby town; its chapel had been converted into a dressing station and stretcher bearers slept in shifts between the altars. 'Everything', she wrote, 'is unutterably sad and awful.'

28.3.18: Thousands coming in day and night. We are in the theatre from 7 a.m. till 8 p.m. then work in the Chapel attending to the new admissions till any hour in the morning.

3.4.18: On duty in theatre yesterday till 10 p.m. then in resuscitation hut till 8 a.m. This work is very depressing. There is not sufficient time to do all that the boys need. The huts are all so full and the boys so helpless and so sick — it seems as if the end of things will never come.

9.4.18: No time for anything but work… Last night Sister Gascoyne and I were on duty in the Chapel and we had 1000 men badly gassed brought in. Poor fellows how they suffered… Those of us who are working among the gassed men have lost our voices — and can just about manage to whisper. This is unfortunate for the men seem to like us to talk to them.[27]

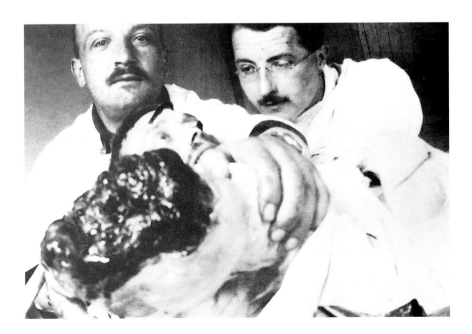

Figure 2.8
Sister Hilda Loxton sent this photograph home with the message: 'These are the wounds we have to deal with.'
(AWM 2 DRL/1172)

■ Was news from the Front usually this grim?

As the battle of the Somme continued, the situation for the Allies worsened. By May 1918, Sister Cook found herself living in a tent on an open field, ordered not to unpack in case she had to move yet again:

30.5.18: All the hospitals between here & the Front are evacuating. Refugees passing along in front of the hospital, driving their cattle & carrying odds & ends of family possessions on carts. Wounded pouring in by the hundreds, — the receiving room full to overflowing — one long line of ambulance outside the hospital, disgorging & taking off, others flying in at the gates covered in dust. Up all night going hard.

31.5.18: An awful day. Rushed to tears — poor devils very badly wounded.

1.6.18: Another and worse day. Wounded pouring in — up till midnight getting dressings done — an air raid going strong during the din — dropped bombs on the Compeigne road about a mile away.[28]

Six weeks later, Sister Cook's casualty clearing station was the only one left along that section of the line; all the others had been evacuated. The dead and dying lay all around her:

16.7.18: The hospital crowded with badly wounded lying on stretchers on the floors, in between the beds, tents hastily erected, — packed with very bad cases — and getting very little attention. After we had finished our work we went into one tent & found it full of wounded who hadn't had anything to eat or a drink for three days. Our own tents — our old sleeping quarters — were full of boys who couldn't live long & weren't even operated on.[29]

Not even sleep offered any escape from this nightmare. Exhausted nurses fell unconscious only to dream of the wounded. Others could not close their eyes for the horror that surrounded them:

Today I had to assist with ten amputations one after the other. It is frightfully nerve-wracking work. I seem to hear that wretched saw whenever I try to sleep. We see the most ghastly wounds and all day long are inhaling the odour of gas gangrene. How these boys suffer![30]

Perhaps the most frightening aspect of work at the clearing station was its unremitting speed. Patients were operated on and sent down the line all within the space of 24 hours. Beds had to be cleared to make room for others. In conditions like these, nurses could not establish any relationship with their patients — they became poor boys, nameless lads, one face merging into another in a sea of human suffering. Time and again, nurses lamented being able to do so little for their patients. There was little time to comfort and even less time to listen.

In the base hospitals, however, relationships with the patients became much more intimate. In the long and painful weeks of treatment, nurses tended far more than men's physical wounds. They soothed, encouraged and reassured their patients, waking them from nightmares where 'they lived through all their awful experience again', reminding them of home and friends and family.[31] Some 'boys' were especially dear to them, perhaps because they were little more than children:

I have in my hut several very young boys (baby soldiers we call them) there's a wee Jock [a Scot, by the name of] Brees, with his right arm gone and the muscles of his chest badly lacerated. He looks such a wee boy and when I ask him what is keeping him awake he tells me he is a wee bit too tired to sleep. Baby 2 is a little scrap of a boy named Hancock with a bad abdominal wound. He certainly doesn't look a day over 14…baby 3 is a Stratfordshire lad named Dart with a tremendous wound in his back. When this wound has to be dressed the corporal holds him up in his arms. The poor little chap cries piteously when we go to do him.[32]

Document 2.7

A soldier's gratitude

Sister,

The accidents of war made me your patient & you my sister for a period of 4 months. During that time you have done all you could to make me comfortable & repaired a damaged hand. I cannot find words sufficient to thank you for all your kindness. It was my good fortune to be a patient in B2. I hope you will excuse my impertinence (being a married man) for writing this to you but I would always regret it if I left here without giving you some acknowledgment for what you had done. You may not know it 'but I do' — every patient that has entered your ward has not been there long before he has passed the remark (I'll give you it in soldier's language): I have dropped on my feet — that sister is just IT.

May your future give you as many joys as you have given to others here, God Bless you.

A.D.

(Laura Grubb Papers, PR 83/40 (6), Australian War Memorial)

Oranges and Lemons

Figure 2.9
(Ms 3637, National Library of Australia)

■ Soldiers responded as best they could to the care offered by their nurses. Many continued to write to them long after they had been invalided home. Why do you think Sister Grubb chose to keep this particular letter?

■ What is this sketch by a soldier patient saying?

Not surprisingly Australian nurses became particularly attached to soldiers from their own country. The diggers were *their* boys, their broad accents brought back memories of home — their uniforms, sometimes even their faces, reminded them of the brothers and loved ones who fought beside them. During the bloody retreat from Amiens, Elsie Tranter confided to her diary:

We three Australians are very glad to be here. Such numbers of the diggers have said how nice it is to have someone from their own country here. Needless to say we are all tremendously proud of our own Aussie boys. They always seem to be the nicest, the bravest and the most humorous of all. But then perhaps it is just because they belong in a special way to us.[33]

It was particularly hard for the nurses to lose those boys who 'belonged' to them. It was nurses who held the hands of the dying, who wiped the cold sweat from the brow and bent down to hear men's last faltering messages. And to nurses fell the task of writing to their loved ones:

I have many 'last' letters to write now to mothers in Australia and New Zealand. Many of the boys have entrusted me with very precious messages. They were game to the end.[34]

Document 2.8

The gratitude of soldiers' families

Dear Sister Grubb,

I want to thank you so much for all your kindness to my Dear husband. It would be a great pleasure to me if ever the opportunity came to thank you personally. Our home is small but clean and comfortable and you would be sure of a hearty welcome. When we first got word of my husband's wounds my little girlie aged eight said Mother shall I pray that Daddy will have a good kind nurse? My girlie's prayers were answered through you. By the description my husband gives of you I am sure our patients will ever remember you. I am so sorry that you should lose your dearest one this terrible war. May God ever guard and keep you. It was the greatest joy of my life to get my husband home again. It does not worry me that he can't use his right hand. I think he was most fortunate to get home as he did. He is now looking more like his old self. I trust you are enjoying the best of health. May God bless you in your noble work.

    I am sincerely
    Yours
    L. Davison

Dear Miss Grubb,

    Thank you so very much for your kindness in writing to tell us of the way in which my dear brother died. It was a great comfort to us all to know that he had every care and attention and that so much was done to try and save him. At the same time it was a great grief for us to know that it was all of no avail. We were looking forward so much to his home-coming, especially as the war was so nearly over, and we can't realise that we shall never see him again.

    You very kindly offered to tell us anything that we would like to know about his illness. We should be so grateful if you could tell us whether he knew there was no hope for him & whether he sent any message or if he spoke about any of us while he was ill. Also could you tell us what were the complications of which you spoke.

    Any small detail will be of the greatest interest to us, as we all thought so much of him. Thanking you again very much for your great kindness and hoping to hear from you again.

    Yours very sincerely
    A.A. Turville

(Laura Grubb Papers, PR 83/40 (6) Australian War Memorial)

■ **What insight do these two letters give us into the role nurses played in helping the families of dead soldiers?**

■ **How do you think nurses would have felt writing and receiving such letters? Was it part of their job?**

Nurses on the Western Front were also exposed to considerable personal danger. Most of the medical stations were situated within a few kilometres of the line. By day, nurses heard the steady beat of Lewis Guns; by night, the sky lit up with flares and artillery. The hospitals and casualty clearing stations were often within range of the 'Big Guns' and, positioned on major transport routes and near training camps and munition dumps, they were obvious if not always intended targets.

Bombing raids were also common. Just a few days after a gas attack opposite them, Hilda Loxton and her companions found themselves the target of an air raid:

Figure 2.10
Sister Ada Smith close to the Front at Trois Arbres
(AWM P0156/81/66)

■ What shelter or comfort would this tent offer in bad weather?
■ What function did the duckboards perform?

Figure 2.11
Several nurses and patients were killed when a German bomb was dropped on this Red Cross Hospital at Etaples, in France.
(AWM HO9726)

■ Why do you think the hospital was bombed?

Our hospital levelled by the Hun machine that came over. Perfect moonlit night. Heard the bombs exploding... [One fell] just a few yard from our sleeping quarters where 12 sisters were in bed, debris fell all over the roof, showered like hail stones... [Another blast] cut through the pillows, streaming feathers all over the place...smashed up the screens and all the glass cases... [The] worst injured was Sister Tefrey, a young Canadian nurse 23 years of age. She was on duty...when a large piece of red-hot shrapnel...struck her feet, completely blowing away her heel.[35]

Australian nurses showed extraordinary courage in these circumstances: they continued to work under fire and risked their own lives to help the injured.

Much is made of the comradeship of men in wartime, of the intense friendships which form, and the loyalty of men to their mates. Nurses, too, formed close relationships with each other which helped them cope with the strains of their work and gave them courage in times of danger:

Yesterday's 'Times' has given a great account of our flight from Grevillers but truth to tell it was not all through that pet phrase of the press 'devotion to duty' that we kept on working while the shells were screaming round. It was really much easier to keep on working than not — Being with others made us feel safer. You can't face these things alone — but with a pal beside you, you feel strong to face danger.[36]

Facing danger was not the only thing which made nursing difficult. Highly trained and extremely dedicated, nurses had to cope with the inefficiency of Army hospital management, a system which seemed more concerned with maintaining military hierarchy than relieving the suffering of the sick and wounded. Tevie Davies wrote to her mother:

Their hospital ways are not our ways...our systems excel any that I've come across yet... Here an order passes through at least three hands before being carried out, whereas we would have it through almost at once.[37]

When Australian nurses were given more freedom in the wards, the comfort of patients and the general standard of care improved enormously. The Army was reluctant to allow the nurses too much responsibility but sometimes they had no choice. For example, at the height of the Somme offensive there were not enough doctors to cope with the incoming wounded and nurses had to hurriedly learn to administer anaesthetics. This they did with enthusiasm. With pride in their new skill, they performed under great pressure, often struggling to keep awake against the effects of the chloroform fumes — which they also inhaled. Yet as soon as the rush was over nurses were sent back to their wards and doctors reclaimed their old territory. Months of study and thousands of successful operations had not succeeded in raising women's status in the Army.

The militarisation of nursing was equally resented. Badges of rank were introduced, reminding the nurses that they were honorary officers. Time and again, senior medical staff and the Army Command intervened to prevent nurses 'fraternising' with

Document 2.9

Military bureaucracy

To get a tooth brush you have to give the name, rank, regiment number, service, age, and any other old thing you can make up and then sign it and get the patient to sign it send it down to the ordinance store and then as likely as not they will send it back and tell you you have not put the number of the bed on the ward or some other damned thing and then finally it will go down again only to find they are out of them…and you wonder where the millions of pounds are going that Australia alone is sending…

(Letter from Narelle Hobbes to 'My dearest Smithkins', 26 July 1915, 57/1, Australian War Memorial)

■ Narelle Hobbes was stationed on the fortified island of Malta. What does her account suggest about the frustrations of Army nursing?

■ How does her situation compare with **(a)** a sister stationed at a large base hospital in France and **(b)** a nurse serving in a casualty clearing station near the front line?

their patients. But military hierarchy was alien to the task of caring for the wounded; it also offended the democratic outlook which came to characterise Australian nurses and soldiers. Like many of her companions, Elsie Tranter resented the stiff authority of British officers and their treatment of her countrymen:

There is one man I <u>hate</u> here and that is Captain Grieve…the surgical specialist. He hates the Aussie boys so much — as much as I hate him. Last night I lost what little respect I had for him. There was not much to lose. I was on duty since early morning and that particular operation was the 24th I'd assisted at for the day. Capt. Grieve knocked down some forceps. Muttered something I didn't hear so he swore at me, swore at the unconscious patient and at the orderly. Our Aussie boys, whom he despises, may be able to hold the premier fashion anywhere for their extensive and illustrative vocabulary — but to their credit keep to reasonable limits when there are women folk about. But of course Capt. Grieve is not a rough digger but an educated English gentleman…horrid![38]

In trials such as these, Elsie Tranter had the support of both her fellow nurses and her patients. On the Western Front, as on the Gallipoli Peninsula, Australians found strength among each other: they were 'mates', they 'stuck it out together'. But other Australian women serving abroad were not so fortunate.

Figure 2.12

Hilda Loxton and others in slit trench, Essay, 1917
(AWM PO 1790.002)

■ What effect would such military precautions have had on nursing work?

■ Why were they seen as necessary?

■ Working in the British hospitals was bad enough; the 21 Australian nurses who served with the French faced additional challenges. In what ways was the situation of a Red Cross nurse more demanding than that of an Australian Army sister?

Document 2.10

Nursing for the French Red Cross

12.9.1916: Reached Marseilles at 10 am — Cannes at 1.15 pm. Drove Gallia Hospital — a large Hotel facing the sea front. Very down hearted & depressed at the State of things here — our first dinner with the Staff awful — had to quit hurriedly & go to the Hotel for dinner. Walked around the sea beach after with two of the English Sisters — also two Canadians here.

13.9.16: Went on duty to the large Second floor wards — in the Salle de Pansements — dressing rooms — where I'm to be installed. French Hospitals are very queer & amazingly badly off for properly trained people. 60 patients in my ward. Found my lack of the French tongue most trying.

(Cook Diary, PR 82/40, Australian War Memorial)

Forgotten outposts: India and Greece

Figure 2.13

Washing day in Salonika
(AWM CO4337)

■ What does this photograph tell us about a nurse's 'duties'?

In many ways a posting to India or to Salonika was a profoundly disappointing experience. The 500 nurses sent to India and the 300 who served in Greece had joined the Army to help Australia's war effort; instead they found themselves nursing almost every imaginable nationality but their own, and dealing mainly with sick rather than wounded patients. They also resented the view held by some people at the time that they were having an easy time of it while their colleagues at the Front were doing the real work.

There was no actual fighting in India: the only wounded the nurses saw were men shipped across from Mesopotamia. Salonika was closer to the fighting. Greece was an ally of Britain and pitted its tiny army against Bulgaria and Turkey. But such skirmishes were seen as incidental to the 'real war' raging in Europe. The campaigns in Greece were even more poorly resourced than the shambles we have seen in France and Turkey. In the hills around Salonika, Sister Laura Grubb learnt the meaning of hunger:

Thursday: For breakfast, — a suspicion of porridge, [inedible] salt bacon and biscuits which again refused to be broken. This has been the iron ration from one morning until next. For lunch, bully [bully beef, or corned beef] and, wonder of wonders, pickles and dry bread…to follow. If only they would give us a little butter and jam to fill up on it wouldn't be so bad but the small ration of bully and dry bread and cold water to wash them down are not enough to satisfy. The exercise we get and this hunger are almost unbearable.[39]

Equally unbearable was the landscape. Far from the lush hills of Tasmania, Laura Grubb found herself in a dry, treeless land, 'the most terribly hot and dusty' place she could imagine. Here, as in India, the nurses found few social diversions. There were no outings to Paris, no leaves to London; indeed, for most of her time, Laura was confined behind a barbed wire compound. Travel was unsafe and much of her pay was spent supplementing her own rations and those of her patients. And how her patients suffered:

Wednesday: Convoy in today, about 23 patients, poor boys. If only the people at home could see the injustices meted out to these lads the whole world would be up in arms at their treatment — broken legs, broken arms, wounds still discharging, dismissed from Hospital within a few weeks of admission to go back up the line and malaria and dysentery raging, only to be sent back again physical wrecks for a few more weeks in Hospital then at it again — worked like dogs until they drop in harness then not even sent home — detained for light duty… It fairly breaks one's heart and we are so helpless and they, poor lads, so grateful.[40]

Dysentery and malaria were difficult to treat: in the early twentieth century, medical science was ill equipped to deal with such diseases. But in both Greece and in India Australian nurses protested that many deaths were avoidable:

If only this…awful Imperial Government…would leave us alone we could do so much more for the lads' comfort but all our time is spent writing little bits of paper and then getting them signed for the absolute necessities…[41]

In Australia Laura Grubb had prepared herself for extremes of cold, heat and even hunger — most of the hardships were to be expected. It was the loss of faith she found so difficult to deal with. The 'mother country' had abandoned her children:

A little nourishment last night but I feel so helpless…one poor chap very sick, I'm afraid we are going to lose him. Oh, the wickedness of dying out here away from everybody, being buried in that little cemetery that is fast filling up and clad only in a grey blanket for which their people at home pay 4s 6d…poor [boys], how little they knew what they were coming to.[42]

■ What does Sister Davies find so objectionable about the English in India?

■ Why do you think she writes about the wattle immediately after she has been discussing the deferential English 'tommies'?

Figure 2.14

Australian officers and nurses picnicking at the 'Spinney', Ismalia, Egypt (AWM JO5885)

■ Did enlisted men have the same opportunities for social diversions with the nurses?

Document 2.11

The English in India

Australian nurses were often appalled by the British Army. As Evelyn Davies saw it, the English 'imperialists' were at their worst in India.

11 October 1916: We miss looking after Australian men awfully, there is something totally different in the English Tommy [ordinary enlisted man] — even the Territorials are not free at all. Poor things — even when they are fearfully ill they stiffen at the sight of an officer and it's 'Yes sir, or no sir'. Our boys are perfectly natural and game — no giving in with them. Poor Tommies are quite a secondary consideration, [they are] taken collectively, never individually. My word Mum, the last wattle you sent was wonderfully fresh and the scent was quite strong. I loved it so did the others…

17 October 1916: Life for the Tommy in India is very hard. In the out-stations only women of the domestic servant type and nurse girls associate with them and, as most of the servants are natives, they fall back on Eurasians for never would an officer's family deign to speak to a Tommy. The class distinction among the Imperial people is most marked. It is wonderful in this station to notice the different circles of friends, each class depending on the height of rank… English people are not free or natural like we are. You have no idea how awful it is to have to be strait-laced always. Still, I'll make up for it when I go home…

12 November 1916: I hope another year will see peace and rest once more. I am just longing to come home again to live among people with homely honest feelings, not those who are all gush and outside show.

(Letters of Sister Evelyn Davies to her mother, 3DRL 3398, Australian War Memorial)

The time spent on these forgotten frontiers was not always so tragic. Here, as elsewhere in the war, nurses developed warm and caring relationships with their patients. Through humour, chitchat, sometimes romance, they overcame the loneliness. Fraternisation with the men was also a way of defying the military authorities, of declaring that one was not a servant or a number but a person, an individual. But as a form of rebellion it was dealt with accordingly.

Scrutiny of the nurses' behaviour was particularly harsh in India; the pettiness and snobbery of Anglo-Indian society permitted no social relationships between 'men' and 'lady officers'.

Deolali case study

At Deolali in 1918, five members of the Australian Army Nursing Service were accused of immoral behaviour and an official inquiry held into their conduct. The charges ranged from the petty to the ridiculous. One sister was accused of walking beside a lieutenant at 10 o'clock in the evening; another, a married sister, was allegedly seen in the arms of a sergeant; a third was supposed to have had sexual intercourse with a Turkish sweeper on the floor of the ward.

All the charges were based on the evidence of one man, an Italian officer who had been employed by the camp commandant to spy on the women. The inquiry found the nurses completely innocent.

This extraordinary vendetta against the Australian nurses seems to have been retaliation for their disregard of the unwritten rules of social conduct. In particular, two off-duty Australian nurses had, some time earlier, spoken to a non-commissioned officer while having afternoon tea at a lodging-house run by another non-commissioned officer's widow. As Surgeon-General Fetherston noted:

Speaking to a Non-commissioned Officer, which in the eyes of many Imperial officers, is an unpardonable sin, and not being able to prove anything against these two nurses, the Camp Commandant started a foreign spy to work, who to show his zeal and acumen trumped up some cases and told lies.[43]

Not surprisingly, the nurses felt very disillusioned by this episode. Having volunteered their services and risked their lives for the sake of the British Empire, it came as quite a shock to be persecuted in this way by supposedly 'decent Britishers'.[44] The action also had the opposite effect to that intended by the authorities — if that was the way 'officers and gentlemen' behaved, the nurses could hardly be expected to admire them or wish to follow their example.

■ What are these two pieces of verse implying about the behaviour of nurses away from the matron's eye or under cover of darkness?

Figure 2.15
Australian nurses outside King George War Hospital, Poona, India
(AWM AO1178)

■ Why was 'keeping up appearances' seen as essential in India?

Document 2.12

Illicit romance

The wartime papers of Sister Laura Grubb include a little folder called 'The Swankers'. It contains two photos of her — one with another nurse and a Tommy, the other with a Tommy on either side. Beneath the first photo is the following short poem.

> Three little swankers
> Sitting on the brink
> Absolute spankers
> Looking in the Pink.
>
> Caring not a jot
> In that lonely spot
> There to roam or 'lie'
> Free from Matron's Eye.
> D.G.S.

Also in these papers is a sketch of a uniformed nurse about to climb onto the bed of a soldier patient, with the following verse underneath.

The Night Sister
The ward sister on in the night time,
Gets pity for missing the sunshine,
But take it from me,
It's a jolly old spree,
'Thumbs up Boys' says Tommy at light time.

(Laura Grubb Papers, PR 83/40 (6), Australian War Memorial)

Ending the madness: Armistice

The Great War ended in November 1918. In the last few months, the Allied and German armies moved further and more quickly than they had at any other time in the conflict. Trench warfare ended but this brought little relief to either the soldiers or the nurses. Attacks and counter attacks, advances and evacuations — all placed enormous strain on energy and resources.

And the war became increasingly dangerous for the civilian population. Roads and railways were cluttered with refugees, often caught in the crossfire of the two opposing armies. Many fled toward the hospitals, hoping to find aid and shelter. In their letters and diaries, Australian nurses wrote of this new tide of human suffering:

10.4.18: Every evening now about sunset the civilians from the town come into our grounds and settle down in the tunnels for the night. It seems cruel that civilian women and dear little innocent children should be exposed to so much danger and have to endure so many hardships.[45]

Document 2.13

Refugees

In March 1918, a contingent of Australian nurses was evacuated to a Canadian hospital at Doullens.

Our journey…was not a pleasant one. We passed several batches of German prisoners at work on the roads. They looked quite jubilant. As we passed through Albert, the last of the civilians were leaving it — old people, tiny children, all making their way to a safer place, taking with them what few belongings they could. One family we saw resting on the roadside, one tiny child asleep on the baggage and a little girl about 10 years standing with her hands on her hips looking back towards the home they had been forced to leave — a look of defiance and hatred on her face. Scenes like this will live forever.

(Tranter Diary, 22 March 1918, 3DRL 4081, Australian War Memorial)

■ Why do you think the memory of the little girl was so important to Elsie Tranter?

Eventually, the Allies were able to drive the Germans back and the nurses were on the move again, this time advancing across the devastated battlefields that had once been peaceful farms and villages:

27.9.18: Before rising in the morning I and five others were told…to be ready at 9 a.m. but actually did not leave until 1 p.m. It is a drive of fully 50 miles through Frévent, Doullens, Albertour near Bapaume. Immediately after leaving Albert the terribleness of the battlefield strikes one, going through villages one would never guess were such unless pointed out to you. Instead one sees everywhere crosses — British soldiers mainly, who have given up their life. Here and there German signs are to be seen. The front car broke down so we went and investigated — the ground full of shell holes, graves, carrying many war souvenirs. In one place the skull and remains of a poor British Tommy was seen.[46]

It seemed as if the landscape had been 'tortured' by war, and every inch of ground soaked with the blood of soldiers. Finally, the end came. Nurses, civilians and soldiers alike were overcome by a sense of joy and relief, anger and confusion:

Armistice. At 11 am. Church bells pealed out, bugles were blown, guns boomed and France went almost mad with joy. Pourquoi? [Why?] Armistice has been signed. I was unable to go into the town, but those who went said that the joy of the people was beyond bounds. Little children and adults, too, were singing and dancing in the streets, flags were flying from all windows, both soldiers and civilians joined wholeheartedly in the cheering and singing. The French children were well provided with crackers and other fireworks and the adults were so excited they danced around kissing almost everyone they met, first on one cheek then on the other.

Here in the hut we have had a very busy day — such a number of delirious boys. One very young fair-haired boy who has been suitably nicknamed 'Sunny Jim' was practically dying when we went on duty in the morning. When the noise started at 11 a.m. he wanted to know the meaning of it — he thought it was the commencement of a barrage. When we told him that the war was over he seemed unable to realise it and, during the few hours remaining to him, called us frequently and asked 'Is it really over? Won't I have to go back?' He seemed so happy each time that we reassured him. This poor little lad finished his battle towards evening. He was barely 18 years and we were all so fond of him. He was a 'Sunny Jim' to the last. Our day in the hut was altogether rather a heartbreaking one and when duty for the day was finished we did not feel able to enter fully into the meaning and joy of Armistice.[47]

Homecoming

Duty for the day may have finished, but it was quite some time before Australia's nurses would see their home and loved ones. Priority was given to the soldiers they had served, and nurses waited several months for a ship heading for Australia. Many stayed on to nurse a seemingly never-ending stream of patients. One of the cruellest ironies of the war was that it was followed by an epidemic of deadly influenza. Soldiers who had survived the killing fields of Gallipoli and France died in their thousands. And nurses died with them. To this day their bodies lie side by side in green English graveyards — sisters and their 'boys' resting there together.

Even the journey home was not always easy. Many returned home on hospital ships, nursing men mutilated by battle. Others found themselves responsible for the children of Australian soldiers. Hilda Loxton boarded the *Zealandia* in November 1918; with her were 60 badly wounded men, 450 women and wives and 140 babies:

Oh the Babies! They seem to be every where and we were very crowded. We did not expect a trip like this and felt very depressed when we saw our fellow passengers and <u>heard</u> all the babies. Two were only three weeks old...[48]

Figure 2.16
Sisters Minnie Hough and Hilda Loxton (second from left) with soldiers' wives and babies bound for Australia
(AWM P0190 032)

■ What part would the fathers have played in the care of their children?

Sister Loxton and her five companions divided the 140 infants between them. Most of the mothers were very young and lacked the advice of friends and family. The voyage seemed to last forever.

Returning to Australia was an even more emotional experience than leaving it. Most nurses had been abroad for several years; many returned to families who had lost their brothers and sons in battle. As the *Zealandia* rounded the Heads in Port Jackson, Sister Loxton found herself overwhelmed by emotion:

A dear dirty pilot boat sauntered quickly up to us cock-a-doodle-doodling as hard as he could, we hurrahed and waved in answer… Same old familiar sights. Manly boats passing backwards and forwards… Arrived Woolloomooloo Wharf 11am and there saw Reg and Arthur excitedly waving… Band played on the wharf… Hundreds of people waving outside in the street. Sudden rush and they all came onto the wharf. [The crowd] clapped and cheered every one of us as we all came down the gangway.[49]

Hilda had come home to a hero's welcome. But for all the enthusiasm of the day, Australian society was deeply divided. The simple patriotism of a few years before had gone forever. Many people (like some of the nurses themselves) had come to question the sense of a war fought so far away and with so many casualties. The women who stayed behind are the subject of our next chapter.

Suggestions for study

To discuss

1   How did the war differently affect Australian men and women serving in the war zones? Consider such factors as danger, pay and conditions of service (leave, etc.).

2   A young nurse has just completed her training (1916). Several of her friends have already gone abroad with the AIF and she is considering joining them. Discuss the advantages and disadvantages, both professional and personal, which might influence this woman's decision.

3   Assuming this woman went to war, discuss her situation five years after returning to Australia, assessing whether her expectations of the advantages of enlisting were justified.

4   Form of a committee of inquiry into allegations of sexual misconduct by Australian nurses serving in India (see the case study on page 31). Present the cases for the prosecution and the defence. You may wish to call witnesses and the nurses must be given the opportunity to put their own case.

To write about

1   You are a nurse serving with the Australian forces in Belgium. Keep a diary which covers a 7-day leave in Britain and a 7-day period of duty at a casualty clearing station.

2   A dying soldier has left you with a last message to send to his family in Australia. Write a letter to his parents conveying his message and explaining the circumstances of his death.

3   You are a nurse serving on the hospital island, Lemnos during the Gallipoli campaign. Write two letters about your experiences in the military hospital: one to your mother at home in Australia; the other to a fellow nurse (a close friend) serving in Egypt.

To research

1   Using an atlas:
    a   chart the voyage nurses took to war from Melbourne via Albany, Cocos Island, Colombo and the Suez Canal, and via Fremantle, the Cape of Good Hope and London
    b   draw a map of the Mediterranean, marking Cairo, Alexandria, Lemnos Island, Malta and Gallipoli
    c   identify the sites of battlefields and hospitals mentioned in this chapter, and some of the towns, cities and districts visited by nurses while on leave in Britain.

2   View the film *The Light Horsemen* and the TV mini-series *The Anzacs*. How are nurses portrayed in these films? How realistic are these depictions?

WORK ON THE HOME FRONT

3

Paid work

Nurses who visited England were impressed by the range of work performed by British women for the war effort. They were to be seen doing work previously considered 'men's work' — driving ambulances and military vehicles, working in munitions factories and in the fields — replacing the millions of men who had gone to the Front. Women in Britain acted as a kind of reserve army of labour, temporarily filling a need for work created by the war and taking over men's jobs so they could go off to fight.

Figure 3.1
Colonial Ammunition Works, Footscray, 1916
(*Punch*, 13 July 1916)

■ What dangers did women face in a working environment like this one?

Document 3.1

After a hard day's work

The gradual invasion by women of occupations which for years had been looked upon as exclusively masculine has been everywhere increased as a result of the war… Naturally, in Australia, where the manhood of the country has not been so reduced as in other countries, the adoption of farming pursuits by women has not been so marked, but there has nevertheless for some time been a steady, insistent demand for agricultural training for women desiring a life on the land. After giving lengthy consideration to the want and the way it should be met, the N.S.W. Department of Agriculture decided that the Experiment Farm at Cowra should be made available for the training of women farmers. The Department was at the outset met with the question as to the sort of instruction that should be provided — whether it should be merely in the less strenuous branches of farm work, such as poultry-keeping, apiculture, vegetable growing, herb-growing, flower gardening, sericulture, etc., or whether a full training in all forms of farm labour should be provided. Inquiries made it plain that the latter was the tuition most widely sought after… The ability of the women to perform the more strenuous labour of the farm may be doubted by some, but the enthusiastic students who are now undergoing training have shown that in this respect they are little behind the men. As one of them put it after spending some months at Pitt Town, 'Domestic washing and scrubbing is far harder work than ploughing or any other farm operation.'

(*Sydney Mail*, 19 December 1917, p. 18)

■ Why do you think the New South Wales Government was so responsive to the 'insistent demands' that women be trained as well as men for 'a life on the land' at this particular time?

■ What kind of work were the women being trained in?

In Australia, the war had far less dramatic consequences for working women. Because of its distance from the war zones and the hazards to shipping, Australia was not called upon to any great extent for war supplies. Indeed, despite the drain on the workforce as men joined up, some industries experienced a *downturn* in employment because of the wartime disruption to trade links. With men unemployed, women were not generally called on to enter non-traditional jobs. The notable exceptions were farm and office jobs, where women's labour was sometimes crucial in freeing men for military service.

Jessie Barnett was one young woman who began her career in banking in Rockhampton, Queensland, when increasing numbers of male bank officers went away to war. Like other women employed by the bank at this time, she was told quite clearly that her job was only temporary — 'only for the war, until the boys come back'. She was still working in the bank twelve years later in 1928. That year she explained to an Industrial Court hearing how she had previously worked in the office of Dalgety's Stock and Station agency but did not like typing all day. The bank had offered more variety and a higher salary.[1] She later transferred to a Sydney branch of the bank and continued to enjoy her new job. 'I like my work very much', she told the hearing in 1928. 'It is essential for me to have a job.' Like many young women of her day, she was dependent on her own earnings so it was important that her job both provide a living wage and be something she could face working at for a long time, perhaps her entire adult life.

The banks, however, were not very enthusiastic about employing women. They offered work to only a very small fraction of women seeking bank jobs, and these women were employed under very different conditions to those offered to male employees.

Document 3.2

Female employment in a bank

Our company employs girls only through or since the war, through the shortage of men, and their slow return. Pre-war, we could never muster more than four girls. I have a tabulated statement here and I show how many girls left in each year, and the position now as compared with 1918, when the war ended.

1908 was the start. Two girls joined the bank that year, and there were no more until 1912, when one girl joined and one girl left. In 1914, two girls joined and there were no departures. That gave us our pre-war maximum of 4… 1915, the war period commenced. 21 girls came in and two left. In 1916 we took in 41 girls and three left. In 1917 we took in 24 girls and 5 went, and in 1918, our peak year, we put in 63 girls and four left. 1918 was the termination of the war, although things did not come back to normal immediately afterwards…

Our sum total at the end of 1918 shows 154 girls came in and 15 went out, leaving a total of 139… Those girls were introduced under war conditions to enable men to go to the Front… In 1919, we did not take in any girls, and 31 left of the 139… In 1920 our difficulties commenced. In 1920, we took in 20 girls including 10 of those 31 who went in 1919. In 1920, 17 girls went… In 1921, 13 girls entered and 8 left. In 1922, 12 girls entered and 7 left… In 1923, 22 girls came in and 13 went out. In 1924, 20 girls came in and 13 went out. In 1925, 11 girls came in and 15 went out. In 1926, 15 came in and 9 went out. In 1927, 9 came in and 3 went out, and so far, in 1928, two girls have come in and 6 gone out. The sum total of girls who have come to our bank in NSW is 278, and 137 have left, leaving us 141.

(Robert Broad, Staff Inspector, Commercial Banking Company, to the Industrial Commission of New South Wales, Bank Officers' State Conciliation Committee, 1928, Noel Butlin Archives of Business and Labour, Canberra, N112/851, pp. 376–7)

■ Prepare **(a)** a table and **(b)** a graph, showing the number of 'girls' entering and leaving the bank each year, and the annual total of female employees.

■ How would you describe the pattern of female employment in this bank from 1908 to 1928?

Document 3.3

Selecting the 'right type'

No test is imposed on the girls as to stenography when they join. We do not insist on an examination. Bank girls may have heard of a standard being asked for. I do it sometimes as a ruse to get rid of some of the candidates. There are so many girls you have to adopt some reason for not accepting them. There is a very much larger number of applicants than we can entertain and sometimes in the initial conversation I ask them if they have certain standards, and they say no, and I say 'There are girls with that standard to be obtained. We cannot give you employment.' It is only a ruse to get rid of them... I got tired of keeping a waiting list for girls. It got so huge. I do not keep one now. As applicants come to me, if they look likely, I put it on the file. If it gets too cumbersome, I take 20 or 30 off and work from the front again. In those years, I have only wanted nine or six, and what is that out of hundreds?

These applications do not come from a class economically pressed. Some of the girls come from quite good schools — quite a lot come from the Church of England Grammar School and the Fort St. High School — not that there is any discrimination. There is no reason why they should accept sweating rates in their economic position. I give preference to bank officers' children, considering them is priority to any others on the file. It is a common thing that bank officers and managers seek to get their daughters in the bank. We have quite a number...

The bank does not suggest it offers careers to the girls. We have always engaged them only temporarily... [This] shows we have not offered a career for them... Under the officers award girls have certain rates there and to continue under temporary employment was rather a misnomer, but I do not look for girls to stay with us a long while. I think the girls ought to get married and follow the natural course of human life. That is a cause of repeated casualties, with the majority. As to a career industry for girls... When girls of a high standard, higher than the average educational attainment, come to the bank for employment I have at times...discouraged them [from] proceeding with their applications to join the bank... Last year a girl had passed with flying colours at Fort Street School — I cannot recall her name. She had an application. Her photograph was in the Herald. She passed the Intermediate Examination at Fort Street, a higher pass than anyone, with an A in every subject — 9 A's I think. She came for a position and said she felt qualified. I had to admit she was qualified. After a conversation with her I told her I thought she was making a mistake by coming to the bank for employment and that she ought to look for something higher or better than we had to offer, merely these routine positions. When as time went on and she found she had no scope for her ability I told her I was sure she would be disappointed. I suggested a certain course to her. I dissuaded her from coming to the bank because I thought after 6 or 7 years a girl of her accomplishments deserved a better fate than doing this routine mechanical work we had to offer...

There is a Miss Adam at Kogarah, eight years service, £190. She came to us during the war period. She is a sister of our manager at Molong. In response to our suggestion that every effort should be made to let the men go, he volunteered to take a girl at his branch, and he said he had a sister who with a bit of training could do the work, hence Miss Adam went to Molong, combining the position of junior and ledger-keeper. Eventually she came to Sydney at her own request and was given a similar position at Kogarah. At £190 I consider she receives quite the equal of a male for that particular work. I have nothing else to offer her. I have no doubt that the bank, following its usual practice, will give her increments from time to time. If we had a boy there, of course, he would only be there temporarily until he completed a certain period of training, then he would go on elsewhere...

Then there is a girl at Haberfield, the manager's daughter. She joined in Queensland under her father in war time. She was trained by her father. He was eventually transferred to Sydney and he asked could he bring his daughter along too, and we agreed. She is a full-time ledgerkeeper.

There is definitely no progress beyond ledger-keeping work for her in our bank. The male officer is the one who is going to stay with us and accept the responsible work and duties later on, and he should have all the advantages of training...

In the war years women were given employment who were of various ages, perhaps more advanced in years; but for the last five or six years the policy has been to introduce junior girls...

(Robert Broad, Staff Inspector, Commercial Banking Company, to the Industrial Commission of New South Wales, Bank Officers' State Conciliation Committee, 1928, Noel Butlin Archives, Canberra, N112.851)

■ Read Document 3.3. During and immediately after the Great War, what types of women were most likely to be employed in banks, and what kinds of work did they do?

■ Do you think the war made a long-term difference to women's office employment? Why or why not?

Women in some industrial occupations also found their services in greater demand during the war. This was especially so for those employed making men's clothing and boots, and to a lesser extent, ammunition. The Commonwealth Government Clothing Factory in Melbourne, established shortly before the war, took on an extra 150 workers to cope with wartime demands for uniforms. Most of these workers were women.

Figure 3.2
Typists at Defence Department Base Records Office, Melbourne
(AWM HO2334)

■ What are the men in the picture doing, and why is the one standing wearing uniform?

Unemployment

While the war did open up new areas of work for single women in banks and insurance offices, and increase the demand for their labour in some more traditional 'male' occupations, for other women opportunities narrowed because of wartime conditions. Responding to the government's calls on patriotic citizens to exercise thrift, many women dispensed with their 'charladies' and resigned themselves to doing more of the household cleaning themselves. This might have helped the war effort but it was very hard on the charladies, whose meagre incomes were often all that kept their families from starvation. To assist this growing number of destitute women and their families, the Melbourne-based Women's Political Association (WPA) formed a Women's Labour Bureau in January 1915. Its main aim was to find work for these women. After a year of operation, the Bureau reported on its work:

Twelve months' experience of the Bureau has shown us that married women who are compulsory bread-winners form a permanent class in this young and prosperous community. Their husbands cannot, through unemployment, ill-health, drink, or other moral weakness, fulfil their responsibility towards their family. The women cannot go into factories, because they find it impossible to combine attendance there with their family duties. Charing is the only occupation open to them, and now that war economies have set in, employers in many callings and housewives are cutting off 'the charwoman'. This means increased misery for hundreds of families. Through the Bureau we have obtained work in town or country for over 200 women, 90 per cent of whom have given complete satisfaction. We have also obtained situations for the husbands, sons or daughters of other women.[2]

Nor was it only married women who suffered the ordeal of trying to combine paid work with domestic responsibilities. The Bureau also reported on cases of single women, such as one 'young mother, deserted by her soldier sweetheart', who 'put her baby out to nurse while she took a situation and returned to find him suffering from a terrible infectious complaint, and covered with sores. She tried in vain, for more than a week, to get the poor child into a hospital.'

The war also saw an increase in distress among the wives of soldiers. For those whose husbands continued to support them, the war years were difficult. Married soldiers were required to allot two-fifths of their pay to their wives, and three-fifths if they had children. The wives also received a separation allowance and often supplemented this with charity from patriotic funds. Nevertheless, the total amount payable in 1917 was only £1 10s 11d for a wife alone, and going up to £2 17s 9d for a wife with seven or more children. In a time of rapidly rising prices, managing on this amount was by no means an easy task. And rents in the inner city could easily reach £2 a week. Even worse off were those women whose husbands used the war as an opportunity to desert their wives and families. The military authorities were very concerned about this phenomenon, as these comments from the Third Military District indicate:

As can be imagined, matrimonial troubles have caused considerable work in the Pay Office. The cases of married men enlisting as single, and enlisting under assumed names, and those making charges against their wives with the view of escaping from the obligation to allot portion of their pay, have been many. The office has, at times, been besieged with women demanding payment of allotment in such cases…[3]

In the absence of their husbands, soldiers' wives were especially vulnerable to the tactics of unscrupulous landlords, who raised their rents and evicted those who failed to pay. A number of these landlords were convicted under the *War Precautions Act*.[4] It is not surprising, given the economic pressures, that many women were forced to take paid jobs to make ends meet.

However, even working in war-related industries did not make women immune from the effects of unemployment. After production peaked in 1916, many factories began laying off labour. Numbers at the Commonwealth Clothing Factory, for instance, fell from 591 in 1916 to 436 in 1917 and continued to decline as the end of hostilities approached. Workers in ammunition factories suffered a similar fate, and responded with unexpected anger:

RAID ON PARLIAMENT BY UNEMPLOYED WOMEN
EXTRAORDINARY SCENES
Extraordinary scenes were witnessed at Federal Parliament House yesterday, when a number of women, headed by Miss Adela Pankhurst, attempted to storm the House and demand work… [About one hundred women rushed into the House shouting 'We want work. Adjourn the House.' Police cleared them out.] It is understood that a number of the women present had been dismissed from the ammunition works recently…[5]

Unemployed women such as these sought help from the Women's Labour Bureau. This organisation represented not just an employment agency and source of financial assistance for the destitute; it was also the focus of much voluntary work on the part of the women who ran it. Members of the Women's Political Association and other left-wing groups raised money to support the Bureau's activities. For the most part, the Bureau found women employment in the city, but the Women's Political Association also instigated a women's farm at Mordialloc, south of Melbourne, 'to give free training on the land to unemployed and other women'. This scheme secured the support of the Minister for Lands and was reported to be 'an unqualified success'.[6]

Most of the voluntary labour expended by women during the Great War, however, was aimed not so much at relieving distress at home as easing the life of the fighting man.

Patriotic (voluntary) work

In January 1916, Miss Maude Butler donned the uniform of an Australian soldier and marched on board a transport ship bound for the Front. Barely 16 years of age, her 'slight and boyish' figure and close-cropped hair easily passed for those of a soldier. Indeed, one paper reported, only the fact that 'she wore a pair of flimsy boots not at all fit for campaigning led to questioning and the discovery of her sex'. Maude was forced to disembark in

Melbourne where she again attempted to join the Army. This time 'she was bowled out at an inspection of identification disks. Hers were blank.' Undaunted, she tried the same trick in Sydney, marching the streets in soldiers' uniform at the height of the 1916 Anzac Day parade. On this occasion, she was imprisoned for impersonating a soldier, only to be discharged the following morning by an applauding court. But the episode discouraged her from further attempts to join the Forces. 'I can't go to the Front', she told a reporter, 'but perhaps I can do a little good here attending the boys.' Maude Butler served out the war in the YMCA rooms in Sydney, 'a very smart waitress' serving tea and cakes to soldiers.[7]

Figure 3.3

Women marching through Sydney streets with AIF reinforcements (AWM H11568)

■ What other opportunities did Australian women have to wear uniform or bear arms in 1915?

Maude Butler was not alone in her attempt to join the Army. Throughout the war, hundreds of Australian women wrote to the military authorities offering their services in Europe. They volunteered to work in any capacity — as ambulance drivers, cooks, hospital orderlies or office workers. By January 1917, the Australian Women's Service Corps boasted 700 members. The most eager recruits called for the formation of a women's battalion, hoping to shame the men still at home into the fight. But, like Maude Butler's, their patriotism went unrewarded. The AIF was adamant that it did not require the services of Australian women; war was a man's business and women would be 'a liability, not an asset' anywhere near the Front.[8] But unlike Maude, members of the Women's Corps would continue to play at being soldiers. Meeting twice a week, they marched, exercised and studied military manuals. The closest they would come to war was to march alongside junior cadets in a Naval and Military Tattoo held in the streets of Sydney.

Document 3.4

A battalion of women

Just now a Miss Jacob is trying to raise a battalion of women ready to go to the Front and 70 have [already] joined her. It seems absurd to picture these gentle hearted women roughing it with the boys in muddy dug outs and trenches amid all the horrors of the front line. I wondered what prompted the idea until Miss Jacob explained: 'When I went to "The Great Push" [a propaganda film about the Somme offensive] one thing struck me particularly: I noticed a man, and the back of his pants wanted a patch. I thought there is work waiting for the Women's Battalion.' So, my dears, as stranger things have happened, if you find a [strange] battalion coming in from the rear with needles, thimbles and thread, you will remember I gave you an early intimation. Of course, Miss Jacob does not want to advertise other ways of showing good intentions. The Red Cross of this state alone [NSW] send away 6000 shirts, 5000 pyjamas, 4000 pairs of socks and 400 towels monthly…

Vera

(*Soldier*, 10 November 1916)

■ In this account outlining the origins of the Women's Battalion in Sydney, why does the writer find it necessary to trivialise Miss Jacob's efforts?

■ What war work does Vera think women are best suited for?

There were many reasons why Australian women were not permitted to go to war. (The only exceptions, of course, were the nurses who, as we have seen, posed many problems for the military.) On the one hand, they were not needed overseas. Britain alone provided enough women to replace male workers in factories, offices and hospitals and so 'free men for the Front'. More importantly though, Australian men were reluctant to accept any such sacrifice from Australian womanhood. They had gone to war to defend their homes and families; women's place was 'back in Australia', far from the unimaginable horrors of the front line. Of course, women were expected to support the war effort. Indeed, the greatest sacrifice they could make was to surrender their sons, husbands, fathers and brothers to the slaughter. But they could contribute to the war effort only in ways thought appropriate for a woman. Knitting socks was 'ladylike'; bearing arms at the local rifle club was not.

Throughout the Great War, an estimated 10 000 'patriotic' clubs, societies and sewing circles sprang up to provide so-called 'comforts' for the soldiers. Staffed almost entirely by women, they knitted socks, vests, mufflers and mittens, packed parcels of cakes,

Document 3.5

This week I made...

Like many patriotic workers, Bessie Cameron was careful to record her weekly output for the Red Cross Society. This shows her work for part of 1915.

18 June: I have made & cut nine flannel shirts, two suits pyjamas & cut out seven suits pyjamas, knitted one pair sox.

25 June: Cut out eight suits pyjamas & under shirt & made two suits of pyjamas & one flannel over shirt.

2 July: Cut out 6 suits pyjamas & 7 over shirts, made one shirt & 1 pr bed sox. Cut out 7 under & 9 shirts 7 over shirts 1 suit pyjamas & made one over shirt.

16 July: Did the same as above and below.

23 July: Cut out 7 over shirts & made one over shirt.

30 July: This week I made 2 Khaki flannel over shirts & cut out 15 under flannel shirts besides drying 35 towels & packing 3 cases of gifts… & topped all by setting fire to the chimney in my efforts to get the towels dry.

6 August: This week I cut out 12 under flannel and 6 suits pyjamas.

13 August: This week I cut 23 under shirts, 52 yards flannel, 6 suits pyjamas, 39 yds crimea flnl.

20 August: 7 suits pyjamas.

27 August: [Cut] 7 suits pyjamas & made two suits & three pairs bed sox.

3 September: I cut out 6 suits, 3 pyjamas & 8 flannel over shirts

10 September: Cut out 7 suits pyjamas, made two shirts (over shirts).

17 September: Cut out 7 suits pyjamas.

24 September: Cut out 60 yds flannel.

1 October: Cut out 7 suits.

8 October: Cut 6 suits pyjamas, 6 undershirts, 4 overshirts.

15 October: Cut 7 suits pyjamas, 6 undershirts, 4 overshirts.

21 October: Cut in all 86 yards flannel.

29 October: Cut 72 yds flannel, 6 under flannels, 3 over shirts, 7 suits pyjamas.

4 November: Cut 50 yds flannel.

12 November: Cut 45 yds.

19 November: Cut 53 yds.

26 November: Cut 36 yds, 2 doz handkerchiefs.

3 December: Cut 36 yds.

10 December: Cut 23 yds.

17 December: Cut 31 yds flannel, 3 doz pillow slips.

24 December: Cut 15 yds flannel.

31 December: 2 suits pyjamas.

By the end of 1918 Bessie had cut out 4578 yards (over 4000 metres) of material.

(Notebook of Red Cross Work, Bessie Cameron Papers, Ms 12783, La Trobe Library, Melbourne)

■ **What does Bessie's diary (1915) tell us about the nature of patriotic work?**

■ **Why were women thought to be suited to such labour?**

magazines and tobacco and wrote one encouraging letter after another to men they had never had met. It amounted, one historian has remarked, 'to a completely new sector of the economy' and one could well argue it was essential to the war effort.[9]

The largest single society was the Red Cross. Within months of the declaration of war, New South Wales alone boasted 88 city and suburban branches, and 249 branches in the country. The active membership of these branches is difficult to estimate as it fluctuated considerably over the course of the war. What is beyond dispute is the dedication and enthusiasm of individual branch workers. In the small town of Tintinara, in South Australia, twelve 'Red Cross ladies' met each Thursday in the local hall. 'During harvesting we work at home', the secretary reported, 'as we

Figure 3.4
Miss Coll's socks, knitted direct from the fleece of sheep, were packed into bales (left) by the Australian Comforts Fund and shipped overseas.
(AWM H02438)

■ Why was Miss Coll prepared to undertake such (unpaid) labour?

■ Why were working-class people unlikely to join the Lady Mayoress's Patriotic League?

Document 3.6

Office bearers of the Lady Mayoress's Patriotic League

This list of office bearers and committee members features the names of some of the wealthiest families in Melbourne.

(The Lady Mayoress's Patriotic League, *Second Report: August 1915 – August 1916*, Melbourne 1916, p. 3)

The Lady Mayoress's Patriotic League
MELBOURNE.

Office-bearers and Executive Committee,
1915-1916.

President: LADY HENNESSY.
Vice-President: LADY MADDEN.
Hon. Treasurer: SIR DAVID HENNESSY, Lord
      Mayor of Melbourne.
Hon. Superintendent: MISS BEATRICE HENTY.
Hon. Organiser for Branches: MRS. HEWISON.
Hon. Secretary: MISS MARGARET LITTLEJOHN.
Asst. Hon. Sec.: MISS LINDA INGLIS.

Executive Committee:

Mrs. ALSTON.	Mrs. HAGELTHORN.	Mrs. MASSON.
Mrs. ANDREWS.	Mrs. HAYTER (on leave).	Miss BYRON MOORE.
Lady BRIDGES.	Miss HENTY.	Mrs. BYRON MORRES.
Mrs BURRELL.	Mrs. HEWISON.	Mrs. A. ROBINSON.
Mrs. CABENA.	Mrs. HUGHES.	Mrs. SELLHEIM (on leave).
Mrs. G. CHIRNSIDE.	Mrs. JOSEPHS.	Lady SPENCER.
Mrs. COHEN.	Mrs. KEIR.	Mrs. SWANSON.
Mrs. ELMSLIE.	Mrs. LYLE.	Mrs. TICKELL.·
Mrs. GODFREY.	Mrs. McCUTCHEON.	Mrs. WHITING.
	Mrs. McKINLEY.	

Sub-Executive Committee:

THE PRESIDENT, VICE-PRESIDENT and HON. TREASURER.

Mrs. ALSTON.	Miss HENTY.	Mrs. MASSON.
Lady BRIDGES.	Mrs. HEWISON.	Miss BYRON MOORE.
Mrs. ELMSLIE.	Mrs. HUGHES.	Mrs. SELLHEIM.
Mrs. HAGELTHORN.	Mrs. LYLE.	Mrs. TICKELL.

Associated Branches	...	...	number 54
Work parties contributing	...	...	,, 201
Brigade Depôts recognised, for Shipments		,,	17

cannot spare time to meet [and we] have such long distances to drive.' Even so, these women sent a steady stream of comforts to the main depot in Adelaide. In a few months they despatched to Government House: 251 suits of pyjamas, 133 handkerchiefs, 51 bed shirts and trousers, and 21 pillows, along with 48 dozen eggs, 'numerous pounds of butter, vegetables, cakes, poultry, scones, biscuits and various tins of food'.[10] Other women appear to have devoted themselves to the singular pursuit of knitting. In one year alone Ruby Wallace, a 13-year-old student at Edinglassie in New South Wales completed 100 pairs of socks, three balaclava caps, four vests, 30 pairs of mittens, 80 pairs of bootees and 20 bonnets. Schoolwork came a poor second to such service to Empire.

As Ruby Wallace's bootees and bonnets suggest, Red Cross work was not directed solely to the aid of Australian soldiers. In the first year of the war, South Australia's Red Cross raised over £13 000 for the Belgium Fund, money intended for the relief of refugees in Europe. 'Belgium', one relief worker wrote, was 'the first claim [on] our hearts...a word of magic which changed all things to gold.'[11] And closer to home the Red Cross and its affiliated societies worked to make the war a little more bearable for those the soldiers had left behind. In December 1916, South Australia's League of Loyal Women entertained 1000 mothers and 3200

■ What does the extract below reveal about **(a)** the scope of children's voluntary work in the city and country, and **(b)** the way that the sexual division of labour distinguished boys' work from that of the girls?

■ How would the social class of a child have affected the kinds of contribution he or she could make?

Document 3.7

'The splendid fighting spirit of youth'

Children as well as women provided unpaid labour for the war effort. This extract is taken from the official history of Australia during the war.

Children were also encouraged to help the fund by doing work. Authentic examples show the splendid spirit of youth. Four boys undertook a contract for street lighting in a small village during the winter months. They bought the lamp glasses and kerosene, and at the end of the season paid their profits, £8, to their school patriotic fund. Two brothers, aged respectively eleven and nine years, borrowed an acre of land from a farmer. Their father stretched the fencing wire for them and they fenced, ploughed, and sowed the soil. From the crop they earned £12, which they paid into the local patriotic fund. A boy earned 30s. by making and selling fly-nets for teamsters' horses. Instances were recorded of school children making brooms, selling rabbit skins, and collecting firewood; others sold eggs, 'gathered

bones, fat, bottles, wood, iron, kerosene tins; they caught and skinned rabbits, trapped foxes, caught fish and frogs and leeches, dug gardens, cleared tracks, cleaned chimneys, swept schools, caught horses, did odd jobs before their home duties commenced in the morning; they gave up holidays, and handed in all their pocket money; and they worked by moonlight when school-work and home-work filled all the daylight hours.' In the city 'the girls could sew and knit, the boys attending woodwork centres could make splints and crutches and chairs. Some could organise fêtes and bazaars and concerts; and of course everyone could bring his or her parents and friends...

There were the military hospitals to visit, and entertainments to arrange for the patients. The League of Young Gardeners was created to swell the war relief fund, by cultivating garden plots at home. From this movement there sprang the three 'flower days', which resulted in raising the sum of £126 354. Next in order came the Young Workers' Patriotic Guild, every member of which had to earn £1 by his own effort.

(Ernest Scott, *Australia During the War*, Sydney, 1936, pp. 734–5) children at a Christmas party on the Adelaide oval. There were 14 trees, 'each decorated with regimental colours' and laden with home-made toys. 'It was a practical demonstration of what ingenious fingers can do', the *Red Cross Record* reported. 'This thought for the children is one way of showing our appreciation of our men who have fought or are fighting for us.'[12] The past tense was quite deliberate. Many of the children mustered beneath regimental Christmas trees had already lost their fathers; little wooden toys must have seemed a poor substitute.

Women's ingenious fingers were put to many other tasks. Domestic skills — usually undervalued by society — assumed enormous importance in wartime. The Lady Mayoress's Patriotic League organised a Thrift Branch in Melbourne, appealing to householders to save newspapers, tins, bottles and rubber for recycling. Wives and mothers were told how to feed their families on less and thus spare every penny for the war effort.

Document 3.8

An Australian Gum Leaf

One form of women's emotional labour was to write letters and poems to soldiers serving abroad. This poem was dedicated to 'Our Happy Warriors' and the proceeds from its sale were donated to the Wounded Soldiers Fund.

Just an Australian gum-leaf,
    Enclosed in a letter from home;
Oh! what a simple offering
    So many miles to come.

But the weary man in the trenches
    Sees with his visioned eyes
His 'little grey home' on the hill side,
    Where the whispering gum-trees rise.

He sees the smoke ascending
    From the cosy fire inside,
Which someone he loves is tending —
    His bonny blue-eyed bride.

* * *

She flies to the gate to greet him,
    With kisses on lips and brow —
The sorrow and heat of the trenches
    Are far from that dreamer now!

* * *

He rises refreshed from his dreaming,
    Strengthened anew for toil
By the little green gift from the homeland,
    A leaf of the 'Fair Dinkum Oil'.

(Muriel Beverley Cole, *Australian Gum Leaves*, 1916, Petherick Reading Room, National Library of Australia)

Like the Red Cross, the Australian Comforts Fund coordinated feats of sewing and knitting. (In total, some 1 354 28 pairs of socks were sent to the muddy trenches of Europe.) It is impossible to assess the number of women-hours that went into this aspect of the war effort. A pair of socks, for instance, takes at least a day to knit. By the fortieth pair even the most patriotic of workers must have felt the strain of it. But there is little evidence to suggest that women resented such labour. Knitting for one of the boys thousands of miles away was something practical they could do to ease a soldier's suffering. Many women had sons, brothers or husbands serving abroad; all hoped to 'do their bit' for the Empire. In effect,

■ What does this poem tell us about contemporary attitudes to women?
■ Can you think of any others (written by women) which might have been popular among the soldiers?

Figure 3.5

*Red Cross members pack
'comforts' for Australians
serving overseas*
(AWM H11579)

■ What type of work in
this photograph was
usually associated with
men, and which with
women?

war work was a way women could relate to the war; it made it all
seem less distant and less terrible. Sometimes, women tucked
letters or photographs or sprigs of wattle into parcels of food and
items of clothing. Messages such as these were treasured by
soldiers, some of whom entered into long and often intimate
correspondence with the sender (Bert Facey, for instance, married
the woman who sent him his first comfort parcels — see
Document 3.9). Others were simply thankful for warm, dry
clothing, a break from the monotonous Army diet, and a symbol
of something kind and familiar. Alas, not all the boys were quite so
appreciative. In August 1916, having informed the *Soldier*'s readers
that thousands of mittens were knitted each week in Sydney, a
woman writer went on:

I only hope that some of you, at least, will recognise our handiwork for what it
is. We have heard such terrible stories of the fate of mufflers and mittens and
other woolly articles being mistaken for pipe warmers or tin holders, or anything
in the world but what they really are.[13]

Organising collectively was an even better way of feeling part
of the war effort. Appeals for clothing or a rush to meet the next
shipment were likened to military manoeuvres; each successful
operation duly described in the journal's despatches. Amidst the
monotony of so much work, the *Red Cross Record* strove to create a
sense of urgency: every stitch, every mitten, brought them one
step closer to victory.

Document 3.9

A gift from home

Dear Sir,

On behalf of the members of this Brigade I have again to thank you and the contributors to the Australian Comforts Funds for the valued consignment of gifts which arrived and were distributed yesterday.

As on previous occasions, the stores have been gratefully received, and thoroughly appreciated by all ranks.

I have also to thank you and your staff for kindness in the matter of forwarding 'Anzac Books' to the Brigade.

C.F. Cox, Brig.-General,
G.O.C., 1st A.L.H. Brigade.
1st A.L.H. Brigade, 29/11/16

Dear Sir,

I am writing from the desert, 200 miles west of Luxor. I left Australia in Nov., 1914, and have been here quite a long time. It is awfully hot; the only time we get any shade is when there is a sand-storm (think of it!), but we do appreciate the comforts sent to us from home; the tinned fruit and preserved milk; and the clean shirts and the fly nets. The men were awfully pleased with themselves the other day, when the G.O.C., Sir H. Hunter, came along and inspected them in their clean shirts and new fly nets. But what breaks the men up is the little letters they sometimes find from the women and the girls, who have made the things. They bring back home when one hasn't had a mail for a long time, and makes one think how well worth fighting for they are.

From a Correspondent

('From Egypt', Australian Comforts Fund, *Lady Mayoress's Patriotic League: Summary and Third Report 1916–1917*, Melbourne, 1917, p. 22)

A few days after the armistice we received some trench comfort parcels from home. Everything was very quiet this day, and a sergeant-major and several men with bags of parcels came along our line and threw each of us a parcel. I got a pair of socks in my parcel. Having big feet — I take a ten in boots — I called out to my mates saying that I had a pair of socks that I would be glad to swap for a bigger pair as I didn't think they would fit. Strange as it seems, I was the only person in my section to get socks; the others got all kinds of things such as scarves, balaclavas, vests, notepaper, pencils, envelopes and handkerchiefs. I found a note rolled up in my socks and it read: 'We wish the soldier that gets this parcel the best of luck and health and a safe return home to his loved ones when the war is over.' It was signed, 'Evelyn Gibson, Hon. Secretary, Girl Guides, Bunbury, W.A.' A lot of my mates came from Bunbury so I asked if any of them knew an Evelyn Gibson. They all knew her and said that she was a good-looker and very smart, and that she came from a well-liked and respected family. I told them that she was mine and we all had an argument, in fun, about this girl and we all claimed her.

The socks, when I tried them on, fitted perfectly and they were hand-knitted with wool. That was the only parcel I received while at Gallipoli.

(A.B. Facey, *A Fortunate Life*, Fremantle Arts Press, Fremantle, 1981, p. 264)

■ These three extracts are about soldiers receiving 'comfort parcels' from Australia. What do they have in common and how do they differ?

■ Compare Bert Facey's account (from his autobiography) with the words of the second letter. How do they differ?

Nothing we can do is too much — give and work, work and give, each according to her talents, trusting that she may be allowed to lessen someone else's pain, aid another's recovery... We of the Red Cross must learn to look upon ourselves as an army under orders, under discipline...and not be turned aside by rumours that this is not wanted or that that is wasted... Try to think what it might be like in the dressing stations and hospitals with the rush of wounded after a great battle, when sometimes a doctor is working twenty-seven hours with no rest. Would you add to his care by letting him lack the necessary dressings and comforts for his patients, or would you add to their pain by withdrawing one single garment, bandage, or food that might help, ease and heal?[14]

■ What resources could Sydney Girls High draw on to celebrate France's Day?
■ Would the day have passed differently had it been organised by a working-class school?

The *Record* was adamant that the real suffering of the war was felt by the soldier — women faced 'no pain, no privations, scarcely

Document 3.10

France's Day

Special 'days' were a feature of patriotic work throughout the war. They were organised to give support to particular causes, and helped to lend a sense of urgency to particular campaigns. France's Day was particularly popular among the pupils at Sydney Girls High School, most of the senior French class having made pen pals of French soldiers.

France's Day was indeed a red-letter day in the history of the G.H.S. We felt that our efforts for the relief of that heroic country were well rewarded when we found out how well we had succeeded. Apart from our work with regard to the Old Girls' stall, the present girls contributed £20 towards the fund. This was raised by having two school concerts. The first the pupils performed in, and for the second we had outside help. For this we are much indebted to Miss Rose Seaton and her pupils, and to the Misses Magnus. At both, sweets were sold. The pupils' weekly collection and the teachers' monthly made up our £20. During the week previous to France's Day, we held Box Day, Egg Day, and Vegetable Day, and France's Day itself we also kept as Flower Day. A good response was made to all these appeals. On Friday our Old Girls' stall was well stocked with articles, fancy and useful. It was placed at the Commonwealth Bank corner in Moore Street. The Bank kindly lent us a room in Post Office Chambers to store things for the stall, which was found to be very useful. Our produce stall was in Martin Place, and did an excellent trade. We also had a coffee stall in Martin Place, which bore such notices as 'Hotel de Kerb', 'Grub or Dinaire', 'Do a Sprat in for France', 'Femme de Charge, Mlle. Caro'. This realised £50.

Among those helping at the stall were Mrs. Britton (Ruth Bowmaker), who was secretary, Mrs. Caro, Mrs. Carver, Mrs. Barnes, Misses Lelia Coppola, Mary Welsh, Fanny Skillman and Leah Marks, as well as a number of last year's senior girls and the present teachers and prefects. The stall was in the charge of Mrs. Garvin. Mrs. Barnes, of Waverley, an Old Girl, was given a lamb by her friend, Mrs. T. A. Tennant. Her son and daughter collected for it, and it was afterwards auctioned. A pig, which was sent by Mrs. Beaumont, of Grenfell, was also auctioned. Miss Dorothy Brunton auctioned a manuscript book of poems by Louise Mack, an Old Girl. We had numerous tins of boiled sweets for soldiers at the Front, but unfortunately these did not sell very well. Those that are left over will be put in our Christmas boxes for the soldiers. Mr. Rendall, the father of Vera Rendall, an Old Girl, kindly donated some original watercolours of views around the harbour. He also gave us a large map of Australia, which was placed on a table near our stall, and during the day was several times covered with money. We had two motor cars in the procession, which were lent by Mr. Hickey and Mr. Armitage, the husbands of two Old Girls. Mr. Hickey's car was decorated in the School colours, and Miss Mary Welsh collected in it. Doris Middleton was also in this car, dressed in brown and gold, and wearing wattle. Mr. Armitage's car collected £26. Collecting in it were his two small daughters, Edna Martin, Mabel Tate, Tamar Lowick, and Fanny Matthews, dressed in white with bands of blue, white and red on hats and frocks. The grand total of the results of our efforts amounted to the proud sum of £360, the old School's tribute to the honour of that grand country, France.

('France's Day', *High School Chronicle*, Sydney Girls High School, September 1917)

Figure 3.6
*Certificate awarded
by the Young Men's
Christian Association*
(Ms 12004, Lucy Family Papers,
La Trobe Library)

■ Why are the snap-
shots described as 'rays
of sunshine'?
■ What are the figures
in the certificate
intended to represent?

any lack of ease or comfort'. But war entailed a very different sort of ordeal for women, an agony (as one Red Cross worker put it) of prayer and weeping, working and waiting. For those whose loved ones were at the Front, the comfort fund group or sewing circle eased an overwhelming sense of powerlessness; one woman remarked that packing a case of comforts put her in a kind of 'spiritual connection with the trenches'.[15] And the circle was there when her worst fears were realised. Women comforted one another when news came of sons or husbands lost; sharing such grief eased the terrible loneliness of bereavement. Wives and mothers were told that their 'fallen soldier' was a hero, that the sacrifice was not for nothing. Indeed patriotic workers were even offered a code of courage to deal with their bereavement. When Lieutenant Colonel Miell was killed in action at Gallipoli his wife set 'a splendid example...attend[ing] at the rooms as usual with her customary inspiring smile':

She stated that by 'keeping up' and going on in the ordinary way she was only doing what her husband would have wished; 'and besides', she added, 'many other women are being similarly afflicted every day. We must keep going for the sake of the boys who need our help'. Similarly Mrs. Seager, when the youngest of her three sons at the Front was killed at his machine gun on Gallipoli, remarked, 'My boy's last words to me were, "If I stop a piece of German lead — be a sport", and I'm going to be a sport. It is only my duty.'[16]

Of course, volunteer war work for women wasn't all a matter of sacrifice and duty. In a column headed 'PLEASURE', a Red Cross journal advised its readers that they need not feel guilty enjoying their work. 'We don't want to be "dull boys", or [dull] women either.' It went on:

Red Cross work is a pleasure in itself. We meet our friends and we chat just as well over our sewing as over a game of bridge, and the constant coming and going to the Circles we work for gives us a freshness of outlook which is excellent for mental and physical health.[17]

Figure 3.7

Ice tableau organised by the Patriotic Fund in Melbourne in 1915
(AWM A05371)

■ Who was most likely to take part in such patriotic activities?

We should not assume that games of bridge were deferred for the duration. In fact, the members of these societies proved remarkably adept at combining patriotic work with many of the recreational pursuits they had enjoyed before the war. Though extravagant entertainment was frowned upon, one could hold a charity ball, a fete, a bowling tournament, even a carnival — providing, of course, that all the money raised went on 'comforts for the soldiers'. For the wealthy, and for those whose loved ones were not at risk, the war was a busy social engagement and a chance to enhance their status in wider society.

Document 3.11

Overheard at the Red Cross tea rooms

Well my dear, I haven't seen you for an age. Where have you been hiding, away at the seaside I suppose. (To the waitress — tea and cakes and scones please for two.) What a pretty girl; this really is a delightful room and what heavenly flowers; I wonder where they get them. I hear this place is paying splendidly, well they deserve it. I don't work here myself, too strenuous, the doctor says I must take things easy, and I've been doing such a lot lately — a month at Southport and there is always something going on there, then a week in Brisbane. I got back just in time for the Charlton Fair — such a success my dear — how do people do it? What delicious scones, I wonder who's cooking to-day. Have you heard anything exciting, I do wish someone would get married or engaged… even weddings aren't very thrilling these days. Look, there is one of those new pleated cretonne skirts. It would be smart if the wearer didn't weigh 14 stone. I see there's a party to-day

— I wonder whose it is — the table looks sweet.

There's Mrs. P… She's tremendously keen on the elections I hear. Everybody is talking elections in Brisbane and they all say they're sure to be in March, and what about the Early Closing Bill, I wonder — I'm sure I shouldn't mind if the hotels never opened at all, but some people seem to mind dreadfully. Oh there's Miss S…, such a patriotic war worker, and by the way have you heard there has been a regular shuffle in the Funds? The Red Cross are moving out of their room in Ruthven Street and going, I'm not quite sure where, and the Sock and Comfort are moving higher up the street. The Allies' Babies Fund has closed in Toowoomba, so if you're wanting to give anything towards it send it along to Parbury Buildings in Brisbane where the Society is doing good work.

Well I must be off. I'm going to the pictures to-night, one must do something these days, war is so very dull, isn't it? I do wish it would stop — I'm so tired of it and there is nothing to wear one's clothes to — Good-bye and let us meet soon again.

(*Downs Red Cross Herald*, 7 February 1918, pp. 12–13)

■ How does the woman at the Red Cross tea rooms view the war effort?

■ How did the war both expand and restrict women's social opportunities?

Figure 3.8

A CUTTING JIBE

(*'The slacker in our native industries is one of our country's greatest enemies.' – Daily paper.*)

Lady with triplets (to lady with a single): 'Yah! Slacker!'

(*Punch*, 20 July 1916)

■ What point is this cartoonist making?

■ Read Document 3.12. Find each of the places on a map. Are they located in city or country?
■ Why did the various branches pursue such different activities?
■ What purpose did the social gatherings at Victor Harbour and Wayville perform for those who attended?

For working-class women, war work usually added to already heavy workloads. Many workplaces formed special working bees to raise money and make comforts for the troops. Of these, the most famous were the 'Lucas Girls' of Ballarat and the 'Khaki Girls' of Melbourne. Both groups were drawn from clothing workers. The Lucas family company produced fine women's lingerie; the Commonwealth Government Clothing Factory made uniforms for the troops. The 'girls' devoted both their time and money from their limited wages to the war effort:

Two hundred girls employed at the Commonwealth Clothing Factory have formed a working bee for the purpose of providing trench comforts for the Australian soldiers in France. On one night in each week the girls return to the factory after tea, and spend two or three hours in making up shirts and warm underclothing. The cost of the material is defrayed out of a fund contributed to by the girls themselves and their friends. Up to the present, £40 has been expended in this manner...[18]

Later in the war the 'girls' increased their efforts to two nights a week.

Their contribution did not stop here, however. The Khaki Girls were officially formed during 1918 and their activities took on a more public turn. They organised themselves into three branches — a Bugle Band, a Physical Culture Squad and a Rifle Squad — each of which had its own distinctive paramilitary uniform. These groups devoted their time to drilling and performing in order to raise funds and assist the recruiting effort. They travelled widely in Victoria to regional centres such as Geelong, Echuca, Shepparton and Ballarat. In Ballarat they played football against a team of women from the Lucas factory as part of their fundraising drive for an Avenue of Honour. (By the end of the war the Lucas Girls had raised the staggering sum of £10 600 towards the cost of the trees and their plaques.)

The contradictory elements of patriotic work are nowhere better illustrated than in the 'entertainments' provided for the soldiers. In the early days of the war a 'Cheer-Up Society' was established in Adelaide 'to make the path of the soldier as he left Australia as bright and easy as possible'. Farewelling the first of the men revealed Australia's widespread enthusiasm for the war. The public subscribed generously to the function, keen to give a 'good send off' to those parting on a great adventure. In November 1915, 1053 officers and men were treated to luncheon, the officers were presented with gold-plated riding crops, the rank and file 'were each handed a pipe'. And the 'Cheer-Up Girls' made sure that no one was made to feel left out of the festivities:

[One] Sunday...the shade temperature at Morphettville was 111, and a dust storm had turned the camp into a 'small red hell', as a soldier termed it; the Cheer-Ups — 150 strong — arrived with caskets of good things, including oranges and early peaches. The boys had just completed a stinging route march, and were fagged and somewhat dispirited. The Cheer-Ups' visit quickly changed the scene. As oranges and peaches disappeared spirits revived. A soldier shouted 'Cripes, your faces are a tonic to the eyesight, and this fresh fruit is a tonic to the

Document 3.12

Red Cross branch reports, South Australia

VICTOR HARBOUR — President, Mrs. O'Leary; Hon. Sec., Miss Ethel Wright.

We had a busy time on the 8th of this month when we held our Patriotic Flower Show. Owing to the enthusiasm of the workers connected with the Flower Show Society, as well as those of the Red Cross, everything went off with a swing, and the function was a credit to all concerned. Members of the Red Cross Committee superintended the tea arrangements, which were excellent. As usual the people of Victor Harbour gave 'with both hands', with the result that large quantities of cakes, scones, &c., were provided. Guessing competitions, a popularity vote, decorated parasols, and home-made sweets, also a knitting contest, were some of the sideshows, and a tangible proof of the success of our efforts was a cheque for £55 10/, which was forwarded to headquarters. This Circle is now interesting itself in the Red Cross Produce Depot, and this week is sending a box of produce to Adelaide, and hopes to forward one regularly once in every six weeks.

WILLUNGA — President, Mrs. Ward; Hon. Sec., Mrs. J. A. Hughes.

In 1914 a Red Cross Circle was formed, but for want of organising it was not affiliated with the Red Cross Society; therefore, after collecting and forwarding a fairly substantial sum of money nothing more was done, though the ladies worked hard for other patriotic efforts. In March last we received a letter from Lady Galway [the Governor's wife], asking for help, and suggesting that we hold a button day in June. The response to this was enthusiastic, with the result that on June 10 we had £25 for Mareeba Hospital. Lady Galway delighted us by visiting the Circle and giving a helpful and inspiring address to a large and appreciative audience. The Circle was re-formed, with a membership of 33. A meeting is held on the third Thursday of each month, when contributions are collected, also parcels of eggs, butter, jam, preserved fruit, cakes, and other good things are brought in and packed, to be sent to Caius Chambers. Thus far we have sent on four cases. Quite recently a Sock Club has been formed in connection with the Circle, and Mrs. M. Foote was asked to organise and superintend it. We have sent to Government House 20 suits pyjamas, 1 shirt, 5 pairs socks, 2 knitted vests, and 2 parcels old linen. We are indebted to the Broughton Revellers (a concert party of young ladies from Adelaide) for being able to forward to headquarters the sum of £3, and to donate to the Sock Club £2. We have also remitted in two cheques subscriptions amounting to £3. There are thirteen subscribers to the *Red Cross Record*, all of whom express much satisfaction with the fine little publication.

WILLIAMSTOWN — President, Mrs. Robert Ross; Hon. Sec., Mrs. W. T. Collins.

The monthly meeting was held on October 14. There was only a fair attendance, but good work had been done during the month, the Secretary receiving 17 sets pyjamas, 3 shirts, 16 pairs socks, 2 scarves, and 1 cardigan jacket, also 46 garments for the Belgian Relief. Our Belgian collections for the month amounting to £8 8/. We wish to acknowledge and thank Mrs. Murray for gift of 6 lb. of wool. This makes a total of 104 lb. given by our Patroness. It was decided to postpone the floral fair until the New Year, as four events conducted by local committees were being organised during November in aid of war funds, one of these being Repatriation Day, on November 4.

WAYVILLE — President, Mrs. O. H. Stephens; Hon. Sec., Mrs. W. Torode.

It was a happy thought which prompted the holding of a combined fete and bowling tournament at the South Park Bowling Green on Wednesday afternoon, November 22, in aid of the funds of the Wayville Red Cross Circle, and the promoters were rewarded with a big crowd of visitors.

The green lawns were in perfect order, and a wealth of flowering shrubs and masses of climbing Dorothy Perkins and Crimson Rambler roses made a delightful setting. All round the grounds the stalls were arranged in picturesque arbours, decorated to represent 'The Seasons', and the splendid array of saleable goods was quickly disposed of. Setaro's Orchestra played merrily; and there was also the indispensable fortune teller in attendance.

I do not imagine that the men would have attended in such numbers had it not been for the attraction that bowls evidently have for the sterner sex, and it was rather a novel sight to see many uniformed officers of the military forces, their feet encased in sand shoes instead of the regulation boots, throwing themselves heart and soul into the match…

His Excellency was received by Mr. C. R. Morris (President of the Club), Mrs. O. H. Stephens (President of the Red Cross), and Mrs. Walter Torode (a member of the Executive). Mrs. Stephens made a particularly apt speech of welcome, and asked the Governor to declare the fete open. After His Excellency's remarks play began in earnest, and continued until fairly late in the afternoon.

Lady Galway arrived at four o'clock. Afternoon tea was served in the piazza of the clubhouse, the tables being decked in blue and yellow, His Excellency's colours. Miss Madge Parkin presented His Excellency with a buttonhole to match. Little Dulcie Hall and Ross Stephens collected £1 1/4 for flags…

WHYTE-YARCOWIE — President, Mrs. Ley; Hon. Sec., Mrs. R. S. Stacy.

This Branch has been carrying on Red Cross work since August 1915. Meetings are held fortnightly on Thursday afternoons. We have a membership of 28, which is excellent for such a small town. All wool and garments issued are checked and noted. Goods dispatched to Government House are as follows:— 80 pyjama suits, 71 shirts, 52 flannels, 228 pairs socks, 67 pillow cases, 60 face washers, also a large number of towels, handkerchiefs, writing pads, envelopes, mittens, Balaclava caps, jug covers, old linen, cigarettes, bed socks, buttons, ink, pens, tooth brushes, lead pencils, shaving soap, playing cards, tinned milk, tobacco, sardines, cocoa, potted pastes, chocolates, sand bags, also a parcel of books. The school children, with Mrs. J. Walters' kind help, have done much for this Society. Great credit and thanks are due to Mrs. Bryant for her great help in cutting out garments for this Society. Our Treasurer Mrs. Walters' report will show that everyone is willing to help on the cause for the sake of our boys at the Front. Cash received is as follows:— Donations and entertainments, £77 14/3; Button Day, £12 10/; collection at meetings, £18 12/2. Expenditure for material for Society — Wool, £27 2/11; flannelette, £24 2/9; flannel, £11 14/7; Invalid Food Fund, £11; Mareeba Hospital, £12 10/; cash in hand, £14.

(*Red Cross Record*, December 1916)

Figure 3.9

Red Cross workers distribute gifts to wounded soldiers
(AWM H16130)

■ Why are the workers here young, well-dressed women?

inside!' One young fellow, however, stood aloof, and refused to accept any refreshment. Mrs Seager placed a hand on his shoulder. 'What's wrong old chap?' she asked. 'You look down in the dumps.' He glanced at her suspiciously, but the winning smile was too much for him. 'Oh, I dunno,' he replied. 'I feel rotten. Got no friends, and I'm dead lonely; I ain't used to crowds, you see.' 'No friends!' she exclaimed, 'There are 150 friends here at least, all proud and anxious to be your friend, and of any other man in the King's Uniform. Here, girls, come and cheer up this boy.' In a twinkling he was surrounded by a coterie of the white-clad Cheer-Ups (they always dressed in white), and it was soon hard to recognise the morose individual in the merry-faced lad, with his hands full of peaches, cracking jokes with the girls. That soldier shortly became a prime favourite in the camp. It was the Cheer-Ups' way. Show them a soldier who was lonely, and they simply stormed him and jollied him into a brighter existence.[19]

A good time to be sure; but the Cheer-Up Girls also served a more serious moral purpose. Many a mother wrote to the Society to thank them for watching over their children. 'He is our baby [one declared], just 18 years of age, and the temptations of the city are quite unknown to him.' For such young men from the bush, the girls provided 'clean, healthy amusement', an alternative to the pubs and brothels keen on the custom of lonely, displaced men.[20] And the memory of those 'dear Australian girls' was thought to make them better soldiers. On the eve of his departure for Egypt, Lieut. Col. Miell praised their moral influence:

I know that many men in the 9th are better fellows today because of the interest taken in them by the girls of the 'Cheer-Up' Society… All of the boys will fight better because they know they have such treasures to fight for…and I earnestly pray that the mothers of the good fellows will have reason to be proud of [them]. Cairo is the wickedest city on earth, but we are trying to keep them straight… God bless the dear girls of C.U.S…their influence is greater than they think.[21]

Farewelling the boys was an easy matter. The return of crippled and wounded men was infinitely harder. As one Cheer-Up girl recalled: those 'grand fellows', whom the Society 'sent away in the full glory of their manly vigour, return[ed] shattered and nerve-stricken wrecks'. Dancing with the lads had been fun, but how did one entertain the maimed, the blind or those who had been driven out of their senses?[22]

Figure 3.10
Women of all ages and social classes participated in patriotic 'cheering up'
(*Remnants from Randwick* [pamphlet issued by patients at the Randwick Military Hospital], Randwick, c. 1918, National Library of Australia)

■ How does this sketch by a convalescing soldier suggest the visitors had very different methods?

By the end of 1916 a steady stream of wounded were making their way back to Australia. The grand outdoor parties of the Cheer-Up Society were replaced by hasty meals in a hastily assembled hut on the banks of the Torrens. Though it was well furnished and set in beautiful parkland, the Cheer-Up Hut could not have been very cheerful. New recruits, treated to a last lunch before departing for the war, were surrounded by hundreds of portraits of the fallen and tablets recording the names of those who had died since their return to Australia. And wounded men often outnumbered the able. In 1916 a special chair was installed to hoist the crippled up onto the balcony. Intended as a place of light-hearted amusement, the Hut became a haunting blend of hospital, memorial, recreation room and madhouse.

It was also an institution staffed and managed almost entirely by women. The 'girls' of the Cheer-Up Society must have come to doubt the glories of war as they tended to the needs of men made more helpless than children. And there was certainly little glory in the never-ending stream of dishes to be washed:

About 10 000 meals monthly were being served in the Hut, apart from the farewells and similar functions; but we shall later quote even better figures! Reader, you can picture the amount of hard toil which surrounded the operations at the Hut, and the organisation required to keep matters going in apple-pie order. Think of the wash ups, for instance. Mountains of dishes and cutlery were tackled daily by those voluntary workers, after waiting on hungry soldiers who 'took a power of keeping up with'. It was the day by day regularity of the thing that made it so exhausting, and the frequently interspersed farewells and other large functions rendered the task at times simply Herculean. Often a large gathering would termi-nate at 8 o'clock, but the Cheer-Ups could not finish the task of washing and drying the dishes until after 11 o'clock. A farewell to 1000 men would involve the use of at least 3000 pieces of crockery, and 4000 pieces of cutlery and spoons! It was a common experience for girls to be on duty for 13 hours continuously, and they 'stuck it' for years, smilingly and uncomplainingly...[23]

Figure 3.11

(*Remnants from Randwick* [pamphlet issued by patients at the Randwick Military Hospital], Randwick, c. 1918, National Library of Australia)

■ What is this sketch by a wounded soldier convalescing in Randwick Military Hospital saying?

Gender roles

Unlike the Second World War, during which women entered 'male' occupations in large numbers, the Great War seemed to strengthen traditional gender roles. The men went to war, or worked in war service industries while the women performed supportive but generally devalued 'female' roles — knitting, sewing and raising

Document 3.13

Voluntary Aid Detachments

By the end of the war, Voluntary Aid Detachments — VADs — played an important part in the nursing of returned soldiers.

In these days of capital letters many of us are content to take them as they stand, know vaguely what they mean, and not worry about the actual wording. V.A.D. has meant much in England, but in South Australia it is only recently that the military have organised a corps to assist the Australian Army Medical Corps in any necessary work. Mr. G. F. Hussey is the officer in charge from the military, and a committee presided over by Dr. Helen Mayo controls the actions under his aegis, the personnel being as follows:— Misses C. Lord, E. Green, Miller, A. Huddlestone, and Warche (hon. secretary). As their name denotes, the workers are absolutely unpaid, and provide their own uniform: indoors, white pique with white apron, collar and cuffs, with the Red Cross and the letters V.A.D. on the bib of the apron; out of doors, nigger-brown [sic] coat and skirt, with a double-breasted coat and brown buttons, fastening right up to the neck over a stand-up white collar. Pipings of dull red are on cuffs and collar, and the nigger-brown hat has a band piped with red. Both uniforms are most attractive, and the girls are as strict about every point as is the newest second lieutenant with his first 'basqued' coat.

The V.A.s are under military discipline when doing official work, and Mr. Hussey transmits the military orders to them. At present there is only one registered detachment here, the first in the Commonwealth, but another will be formed almost at once. Each detachment consists of 25 members.

Recently three boats arrived in 14 days, and as the chief duties of the V.A.s are concerned with the care of undischarged wounded soldiers, this meant a tremendous lot of work. If the boats go to Melbourne, three women V.A.s accompanied by two men V.A.s who are certificated St. John's Ambulance men, go to Melbourne with a comprehensive kit of comforts for the men, handkerchiefs, pyjamas, arrangements for refreshments, &c., and act as assistants to the nurses. All V.A.s have to pass an ambulance examination, so the workers can be, if needed, of great help to the Army Nurses, and between the two branches the utmost harmony prevails.

When the boats come to our own harbour the V.A.s go down the day before and prepare for their reception. The Harbours Board have given them the use of one of the big sheds, and they arrange for meals, &c. The workers leave town by the 7 a.m. train on the day the boat arrives and two V.A.s go up to town with our own men on the special train to Adelaide. The others remain at the harbour to care for the interstate men who came by the same boat. If the soldiers have to leave, there is not much for the V.A.s to do, but if, as was the case with the last transport, leave is only given for one day, the second day in harbour means real hard work. The V.A.s provide a hot dinner and a dainty tea for the men, and also have a room where they can smoke, play games, write, and hear the excellent concerts arranged by the detachment. The men thoroughly appreciate these performances, and it is found that child performers are a great attraction. A few A.M.C. orderlies from Mitcham are detailed to help and make themselves very useful.

At present the Red Cross is financing the V.A.s, but it is felt that the Central Executive has as much as it can do, so there is great scope for people with poultry farms and big gardens to assist these willing workers in the grateful task of welcoming home our heroes…

In addition to this, their primary duty, the V.A.s go to Keswick Hospital three days a week when medical boards are sitting to decide on the health or otherwise of returned soldiers. The men have to be there when they are wanted, and the hospital authorities do not provide lunch for them, so the V.A.s manage a buffet, where the men have light refreshments.

It will be seen that all these works take money and a great deal of arrangement. Hail, rain, or shine, the workers must be there, and be cheerful and ready to help, whether their hearts are wrung by the sight caused by war's cruelty, or, all too frequently, by their personal bereavement. Sometimes there are 1,400 men to be cared for, and even 900, which is a small load for a transport, is a fair number to provide for.

(*Red Cross Record*, December 1917)

■ Why do you think women joined the service in such large numbers?

■ What social class was a VAD 'nurse' likely to belong to, and was her work as valued as that of the nursing sister?

funds for the soldiers. At one level this is perfectly true. While the war gave British women a chance to take on new jobs and new responsibilities, Australian women had no such opportunities. For them the war was simply more of the same.

But wars are unsettling for any society, even for a country as isolated as Australia. While women here did not enter the factories or form a Women's Land Army to run the farms, the example of their 'sisters' in Britain raised all sorts of possibilities. The women's column in the *Soldier* depicted woman as the new Atlas (a Greek mythological figure), the weight of the world resting on her shoulders. There was, one column noted, 'no sex disability in this war; the women of Britain had proved that they could harvest the fields, unload the ships and manufacture munitions as well and as ably as any man living'. Adamant that 'the Australian woman is made of the same stuff as the ANZAC',[24] columnists claimed a new place for women at the end of hostilities. 'It was improbable that women would be content after the war to be relegated to the back waters of life, in which men have placed her so long. We must act as intelligent human beings and prepare for the inevitable by the organisation of industry.'[25] And this would entail a change in the social as well the economic standing of women. Conservative journals like the *Soldier* found themselves siding with the arguments of 'sensible feminists', and acknowledged that

women have been struggling for centuries to escape from the status in men's minds which regards them as a mere possession, a thing to be catalogued, along with the family bedstead and the clock or to minister to men's needs — domestic, social, and sexual.[26]

It is one of the ironies of the war that patriotic bodies formed essentially to cater for men's needs should find themselves toying with such arguments. Perhaps this was because the work they excelled in was not always 'women's work'. Members of the Australian Women's Service Corps defied all gender stereotypes by preparing blocks of land for occupation by returned soldiers at French's Forest near Sydney. Parties of 20 women felled timber, cleared brushwood and hauled stone in order to make the blocks viable propositions. Women knitted socks, but they also ran successful newspapers. Wives whose own weekly housekeeping stretched to a few pounds collected, counted and allocated hundreds of guineas. Women left their homes to attend nightly meetings in town and city, elected office bearers, discussed politics and debated world affairs in a way unheard of in peacetime.

In all this, women renegotiated what may be called the public and the private spheres. Their organisations were not just charitable affairs; they were also powerful political lobbies. The League of Loyal Women was typical of many. One month it would devote itself to making toys for war orphans; the next it would be holding public meetings to advocate conscription or the early closing of hotels. In each case, women assumed a public prominence that

Document 3.14

The Awakening of Women

They are waking, they are waking
  in the East and in the West
They are opening wide their windows to the sun

For they see the Dawn is breaking
  and they quicken with unrest
As they see the work that's waiting to be done

And their thoughts shall grow and widen
  as each sleeper wakes and stirs
As they throw aside traditions and are free

And the world shall quickly render to the woman
  what is hers
As she typifies the race that is to be.

(*Soldier*, 4 August 1916)

■ What do this poem and the description of the Red Cross procession (Document 3.15) say about the changing role of women in wartime? Did women 'throw aside' traditions and become 'free'?

■ What evidence is there that the war
(a) confirmed and
(b) challenged women's role in society?

Document 3.15

The Women's Red Cross Procession

'Remember this, that there is a proper dignity and proportion to be observed in the performance of every act of life.' — *Marcus Aurelius*.

When the tale of this war is told, the historian will have failed in his duty should he omit the part in it played by the women of the British nation. We may not fight if we would, but we are not denied the privilege of tending and succouring our sick and wounded warriors. They fight for us — we work for them.

The Crusade of Mercy which marched through the streets of the city on Red Cross Button Day was deeply significant — it was one of those actions which speak more loudly and surely than any words could do. It was the personification of dignity — quietly impressive — and the white garments of the women betokened the purity of motive which actuates all who work under the sign of the Geneva Red Cross. At the head of the procession was a band of mounted women, symbolising the Crusaders of old time who rode forth to free a nation from oppression. A brass band was composed of girls from the Burra, who, when their townsmen relinquished the musical instruments for the rifle and bayonet, stepped into their places, obeying the call to 'carry on'.

The appearance of Lady Galway at the head of those on foot…was the signal for…cheering all along the route. No one works more ardently and untiringly than she, and we felt a distinct thrill of pride and admiration as we watched her marching proudly in the vanguard of her army of fellow workers…

Then followed a long line of Red Cross workers, walking four abreast, carrying banners with the symbol of mercy prominently displayed. These included the League of Loyal Women, the Victoria League, the Australian Comforts Fund, the Button Day sellers, Red Cross Tea Room girls, Hospital handicrafts, Cheer-Up Society, V.A.s, and a long line of members of the suburban and country Red Cross circles.

Practical demonstrations of some of the various activities of branches of the parent body were given on a number of trollies. We saw the Government House packing department at work, the 'S.O.S.' (send out socks), the produce depot, men's carpentry section, books and newspapers branch, spinning industry, *Red Cross Record*, Army nurses, and the hospital handicrafts. Each of these conveyed to the mind of the beholder an impression of earnest and useful work…

Such a spectacle could not fail to stir the emotions — it was an illustration of the solemnity, and at the same time of the indomitable spirit which permeates our women as well as our men when there is work of national importance to be done. This noble army of matrons and maids, all seeming to say silently, and yet no less impressively, 'We do pray for mercy: and that same prayer doth teach us all to render the deeds of mercy.'

(*Red Cross Record*, October 1918)

was new to them. In a way, the war created a sort of vacuum in which women could move. When the men were away at war, who was left to march the streets *but* women? This is not to say that women secured equality during wartime. Often, the most senior positions in women's patriotic societies were occupied by 'distinguished gentlemen'. And certainly after the war there was none of the sweeping social change that *Soldier* columnists had imagined. But the war had a complex effect on gender relations; for a moment the accepted roles of men and women were questioned, perhaps even challenged.

The war did not make women equal with men; nor did it make women equal with one another. Patriotic journals claimed that the movement had a 'wonderfully democratic' character. 'Mistress and maid [one declared] have worked side by side doing their bit here while their menfolk are fighting side by side [in Europe].'[27] In fact, social distinctions were very much in evidence. Just as the Army was rigidly divided into officers and men, patriotic societies were extremely conscious of the relative social standing of each of their members.

The Red Cross's patron was Lady Munro Ferguson, wife of the Governor-General during the war and a valued friend of the British royal family. There is no evidence that Lady Munro Ferguson knitted any socks for the boys at the Front or took on a mountain of dishes at a Cheer-Up function in Adelaide. Her vice-regal presence was suited to much better things — opening a fundraising concert, perhaps, or entertaining senior Army officers. Of course, Lady Munro Ferguson made many appearances at convalescent hospitals and spoke encouragingly to men maimed and crippled for the Empire. But at the end of the day, a sleek limousine carried her back to the vice-regal residence, leaving other women to nurse the broken bodies and change the sopping bed clothes.

Inequalities such as these were mirrored across the range of Australia's volunteer societies. How did a gift of a few hundred pounds from the Toorak society set compare with the long hours those women at Tintinara spared during the harvest? And is it fair to ask whether all of the 10 100 'comforts' forwarded by the 65 members of the Vaucluse branch were lovingly knitted by the members themselves?[28] Perhaps just a few of the ladies of Vaucluse 'donated' the work of their maids and servants.

Class was not the only factor which divided the members of Australia's patriotic societies. As the war progressed new divisions were created. Patriotic workers whose loved ones were serving overseas were entitled to wear a service badge issued by the League of Loyal Women. For each son or brother who served abroad a bar was added; the greater the number of combatants, the more 'pride' a woman could show in her sacrifice. A 'little bronze cross' was worn by those whose loved ones had been killed. Just to see one, one Red Cross worker remarked, 'made our hearts beat

Figure 3.12
One of hundreds of certificates signed by Lady Munro Ferguson
(Ms 10332, La Trobe Library)

■ Why do you think such certificates were issued?

high'.[29] Medals such as these introduced women to a military culture; in war men and women's sacrifice was carefully measured and conspicuously advertised.

By far the greatest division was between those who gave their all for the war effort and those who did not. To join a patriotic society was rather like joining the Army; those who refused to enlist were described as shirkers. Patriotic journals advocated the conscription of women's labour as well as compulsory military service for men: in the Empire's hour of need men must fight and women must knit for them. And while women who would not help were objects of contempt, those who opposed the war altogether were met with open derision. War work was supposed to have been an act of love, an attempt to relieve human suffering; in reality, it bred hatred, fear and suspicion.

The way the war divided Australian women is nowhere more clearly seen than in the battles surrounding conscription, working conditions and the cost of living. These issues are the subject of our next chapter.

■ How do you account for the differing attitudes of the girl in charge and the girl in the silk dress?

■ What might make the latter take the war more seriously?

■ Why does the 'old dame' continue to send her parcels? Do you think she is the same social class as the shopper?

Document 3.16

Mothers, wives and sweethearts

A girl in a silk dress came into the depot to ask the address of some soldier in the Battalion and to send a parcel free through the Fund. She got the information she required. 'Are you here every day?' she asked the blouse and shirt girl in charge, 'Yes, of course. If I were not, some 5000 men would not get their shirts and comforts regularly. I wish you could come and help us some day, the men need them so.' 'Oh, I couldn't possibly', said the girl, 'I've got too much shopping to do. But how nice it is for a girl to have a hobby.' An old dame came in next. 'Dearie', she said to the blouse and shirt girl, 'I've got a little parcel here I want you to send for me. Of course, you know my dear boy was killed last November but Dearie they are sending their Christmas parcels off from round where I live…[and] I just thought I'd send one to him too. It's addressed to him the way I used to so…some other boy will get it.'
(A Red Cross Woman, *Soldier*, 29 December 1916)

Suggestions for study

To discuss

1   You are a journalist on a daily newspaper; your partner is a voluntary worker at the Red Cross kiosk in the city. Interview your partner and find out why he or she is involved in this work and how demanding/rewarding it is.

2   Form groups of seven. Each group represents a farming family consisting of parents, three daughters and two sons. The sons are about to leave for France with the AIF. One of the daughters has been offered a place at the State Experiment Farm at Cowra, where she would be taught to do a range of agricultural tasks usually performed by men. She has also been offered a job as a ledgerkeeper in the local bank where her uncle is the manager. The family is divided over which position she should accept. Hold a discussion in which family members put their points of view.

To write about

1   You are the personal assistant of the Governor's wife. Keep a diary of your employer's official engagements for a week in 1917.

2   You are a soldier serving in France during the war. You have
     received a Red Cross comforts parcel with a note inside from
     one of the women who packed it. Write a letter in reply.

3   You are the general manager of a major insurance company
     which is experiencing staffing problems because of the
     enlistment of its male employees. Prepare a statement (for
     branch managers) of the company's policy regarding the hiring
     of women. Be sure to state the kinds of women preferred (age,
     qualifications, experience, marital status) and the terms of
     employment (pay, conditions relative to male staff).

To research

1   Some prominent voluntary war workers are mentioned in this
     chapter. Look them up in the *Australian Dictionary of Biography*
     or *200 Australian Women: A Redress Anthology* (edited by
     Heather Radi). Does their voluntary work appear to be restricted
     to the war period or does it fit into a broader pattern of voluntary
     work extending into peacetime?

2   Draw up a list of charitable agencies which operate in your
     community today. How would this list differ from one drawn up
     in 1917?

3   You may know of elderly members of your local community
     who did voluntary work, either as children or young adults,
     during the Great War. Interview them about their experiences,
     finding out what kinds of work they did, why they did it and how
     they felt about what they were doing.

CONSCRIPTION, INDUSTRIAL STRUGGLE AND FOOD RIOTS

4

While thousands of patriotic women patiently knitted, sewed and packed comforts for the 'boys' at the Front, other Australian women were being equally energetic in other areas. Less convinced of the necessity of Australia's involvement in the war, they expressed their opinions in word and action in an attempt to influence both popular opinion and government policy. In many cases, peaceful protest turned to violent confrontations.

These violent demonstrations were the result of the growing anger and frustration felt by large numbers of the population during the later years of the war. The anger was most strongly felt among Labor men and women who felt betrayed by some of their own politicians, especially the Prime Minister, William Morris (Billy) Hughes. As these people saw it, Hughes had been persuaded by patriotic elements at home and abroad into introducing all sorts of measures in order to maximise Australia's contribution to the war.

Unfortunately, these measures had disproportionately damaging effects on the working people of Australia. Former Labor politicians had severely curtailed the right to free speech and free association; they had failed to control inflation (allowing prices to rise); they had provoked industrial turmoil by supporting new 'American speed-up methods' in the New South Wales Railway Workshops; and, most importantly, had betrayed the Australian Labor Party's policy against the conscription of Australian men for overseas service. All of these issues produced intense divisions within the Australian population and women played prominent roles in the various public debates and campaigns, actively supporting both the pro- and anti-government positions. In fact, the war saw an unprecedented involvement of women in public forms of political activity.

Why was this so? The explanation probably has a lot to do with generally accepted ideas about women's 'proper sphere'. The dominant view of women at this time was that woman's place was in the home, raising children and tending to the needs of her husband. Man's place was in the public arena, earning a living and deciding the 'big' issues for the community as a whole.

Before the war, socialist and feminist women had already begun to attack this gender division: they demanded (and won) the vote for 'white' Australian women and greater equality before the law and in the paid workforce. Many had also challenged the idea that public politics was a man's domain and actively participated in campaigns on behalf of both working men and women. Emma Miller, one of the most prominent Queensland activists during the war, had already achieved national fame for her actions during an industrial dispute in Brisbane in 1912. When a demonstration which included women and children was charged by mounted police, she seized the long pin out of her hat and stabbed it into the rump of the Police Commissioner's horse, causing the horse to rear in fright and toss its rider to the ground. British women such as Adela Pankhurst and Jennie Baines had experience of the militant tactics of the suffragette movement before coming to Australia. For such women, the public domain held no mystique: they occupied it defiantly as a matter of principle, asserting their equality with men.

For conservative women, however, the fear of transgressing on male territory and appearing unfeminine required some powerful force to propel them from their 'ladylike' passivity and domesticity. The war provided just that force, giving these women a socially acceptable reason to break with tradition. War was, by definition, a period of crisis, justifying extraordinary measures in the quest for victory. It is interesting to note the enthusiasm with which so many women seized these wartime opportunities. Respectable middle-class women who would not have dreamt of working in a office for a salary before the war, were suddenly queuing up to do similar work for nothing 'for the war effort'. Likewise, women who would not have thought of campaigning for a political party in peacetime, showed themselves tireless workers in the pro-conscription campaigns.

Working-class women were traditionally less constrained by the artificial public/private divide, but they showed themselves more willing to participate actively in politics because of the added intensity and personal relevance of wartime issues. Supporting vague plans for social justice in peacetime did not have quite the same urgency as stopping legislation that would ship their sons and husbands overseas to die in the trenches. If we are to understand the radicalising power of these years we must look more closely at the major political, industrial and social issues of the time, and women's particular relationship to them.

Conscription

The attempt to introduce compulsory conscription for overseas service was undoubtedly the most divisive issue on the home front during the war. The government made two attempts to have the Australian public approve its plan for conscription, holding referendums on the issue in 1916 and 1917. In both cases the proposals were narrowly defeated, but only after intense and often violent campaigning on both sides which divided the country and split the Labor Party.

Feelings ran so high because what was at stake was literally a matter of life and death. It was not simply that the government and its supporters — the 'pros' — wished to send more Australian men to their deaths on the battlefield, while the 'antis' wished to save lives. Many pro-conscriptionists sincerely believed that *not* to send conscripts would leave those men already at the Front in an even more dangerous position and would possibly also put at risk an Allied victory in the war. For most people the issue took on a personal significance because their male relatives and friends were either eligible for conscription or already fighting with the AIF.

Figure 4.1
(Merrifield Collection, State Library of Victoria)

◼ Why are women and children so prominent in this photograph of the Anti-Conscription League, Melbourne?

The conscription debates also drew on wider, more long-term divisions within Australian society, particularly issues of class and ethnicity. For instance, although the issue did in some cases divide families, in general the working classes, especially their institutions (such as unions, Labor Parties and socialist newspapers)

tended to oppose conscription, while the middle classes (including employers, salaried white-collar workers, large landowners, and almost all the daily newspapers) tended to favour conscription. People of Irish descent were less likely to support the war and conscription than those of English, Welsh or Scottish stock, especially after the savage reprisals meted out by the British Government to the Irish rebels in Dublin in 1916. People of Irish descent found it hard to see the British Government as the defenders of freedom when its treatment of Ireland seemed little different to Germany's treatment of 'poor little Belgium'. The class and ethnic differences were given added heat when prominent Catholic churchmen took a public stand against conscription and their Protestant counterparts actively campaigned for the government.

In all, the tensions caused by the conscription controversy amounted to a war within Australian society every bit as bitter as that being fought in Europe, although at home the main weapons were fear, guilt and recrimination. Women played an important part on both sides of the campaigns — as activists, producing and disseminating propaganda; as newly enfranchised citizens, being targeted by some of the most powerful propaganda; and as objects of both chivalry and fear, providing for one side a rationale for conscription and for the other a justification for opposing it.

Of all the groups formed to oppose the war and/or conscription, the Women's Peace Army (WPA) was the most visible and influential. Founded in July 1915, the Peace Army grew out of a Melbourne feminist organisation, the non-party Women's Political Association, whose members found themselves divided over support for the war. Socialist-feminists quickly fell in behind the flamboyant and charismatic leadership offered by the WPA and, following speaking tours by Melbourne women, branches were soon formed in Sydney and Brisbane. WPA president Vida Goldstein was a beautiful, charming and accomplished woman who had achieved international fame as the first woman in the English-speaking world to stand for election to a seat in parliament. Secretary Adela Pankhurst we have already met campaigning for women's employment. Treasurer Cecilia John was a singing teaching whose famous contralto voice never failed to stir an audience when she burst into any of her extensive repertoire of anti-conscription and peace songs. Indeed, such was the effect of one of these songs, 'I Didn't Raise My Son to Be a Soldier' (see Document 4.7), that it was banned under the War Precautions Act.

Well before the possibility of conscription was raised, the WPA, along with other socialist groups, condemned the war as a fight between rival national groups of capitalists in which workers were merely the cannon-fodder. Women, they argued, should work for peace as they were the 'lifegivers of the world', and thus natu rally more peaceful and nurturing than aggressive males. These women and their supporters felt that conscription was not only morally wrong but would lead to the militarisation of Australian life generally, something which would have particularly unfortunate consequences for the working classes. They argued that conscription would be used as an excuse to introduce cheaper labour to replace men going to the war, and the increased number of troops would be used against any protesting workers. As people attending a Shop Assistants' Union meeting in Brisbane were warned, 'the crowd who were now behind the Prime Minister were the same crowd who [had] called the police out, and even asked for troops to shoot the workers down during the 1912 strike'.[1]

The Women's Peace Army and other left-wing groups (such as the International Workers of the World, the No Conscription Fellowship and the Militant Propagandists of the Labour Movement) were joined in their opposition to the war and conscription by others who opposed war primarily out of religious conviction. Most prominent among these were the Quakers (well-known for their pacifism throughout history) and the followers of Dr Charles Strong's Australia Church in Melbourne, who formed the Sisterhood of International Peace in March 1915.

More sedate and middle-class than their more left-wing sisters, the members of the Sisterhood of International Peace were, like the Quakers, thorough-going pacifists, opposed to *all* wars, not just the current one. Why did they organise separately to male pacifists? While their stated aim was 'to bring the humanising influence of women to bear on the abolition of war', not all its members believed that women were naturally more peaceful than men. Eleanor Moore, one of the group's leading propagandists, believed it 'would be rash to claim that women are by nature kinder and more merciful than men, or less vindictive and quarrelsome. There are women enough to cheer for the wars men make, and to urge men on to the slaughter.'[2] Rather, Moore believed that because Australian women had the vote they also had a civic duty to work for peace and that they could do this more effectively in their own, single-sex organisation.

All these groups joined forces to mount a truly impressive campaign against the referendum proposals. They arranged thousands of meetings across Australia, with speakers travelling from state to state, addressing crowds on street corners and in huge open-air venues when local authorities denied them access to public halls. With the daily newspapers overwhelmingly supporting conscription, the 'antis' fought the propaganda war through a handful of sympathetic journals and a massive quantity of pamphlets and posters, distributing these through the post and at factory gates and popular entertainments. Graffiti was also a popular and cheap medium, with slogans and announcements chalked on pavements and factory walls.

Document 4:1

Australian Women's Peace Army, Brisbane Branch, 1916

What has been the main feature of our Queensland work? It can be summed up in the word 'education'. A continuous effort has been made to interest our women in the problems and causes underlying war, and to face squarely and honestly all the by-products of war, contained in the social evil, unemployment, conscription, etc., with a view to combating those evils.

A scheme is in operation to circularise all the women of Queensland with the objects of the movement, asking for a donation of 1/–. Up to date, a fairly satisfactory response has been made. Members have been enrolled in Gympie, Charters Towers, Townsville, Ipswich, and Toowoomba, as well as country districts out West. Public meetings have been held in several centres of Queensland. Three successful open-air meetings have been held in Gympie, one at the Ipswich Town Hall, and five lectures given in Brisbane by women of the WPA. Literature has been continuously distributed all over the State with good result. A feature of our work is to send delegates to every organisation willing to hear addresses on the peace movement. The women students at the University, the Theosophical Society, the Industrial Council, various WPOs [women's peace organisations], the Meat Industries' Conference, have all received WPA representatives to speak on the different phases of the movement.

Perhaps the most practical effort which has been made by the WPA has been the attempt to introduce new ideals of internationalism and world citizenship into our State schools. A strong deputation was worked up, representative of twelve leading organisations of workers in Queensland, to wait upon the Minister for Education [Mr Hardacre]… The Minister's reply was generally satisfactory. He definitely committed himself to eliminate, as far as possible, the elements of jingoism from the school books, the school papers and teaching. It was promised that the martial atmosphere created in the schools by the kettledrum and bugle should be dispensed with. More economic history should be taught, and the offensive articles in the school papers extolling the bravery of warfare should also be carefully revised or left out. The Government endorsed the position taken by Mr Hardacre and, to further encourage our efforts, an offer has come to hand inviting representatives of the WPA to address a combined meeting of the Queensland Assistant Teachers' Association and the East Moreton Teachers' Association. It can readily be assumed that a direct Appeal to the teachers will be of the greatest value of all.

(Annual Report of the Brisbane Branch of the Australian Women's Peace Army, *Woman Voter*, 15 March 1917)

■ List the range of activities pursued by this branch of the WPA during 1916.

■ Which groups and organisations were willing to listen to the peace message? What do they have in common? What kind of alliances does this report suggest that the WPA was able to forge with other groups in Queensland politics?

■ What does the success of their efforts regarding the reform of schooling suggest about the attitude of the Queensland Government towards conscription?

The efforts of anti-conscriptionist activists attracted frequent raids on their homes by security police searching for 'subversive' literature, and often led to prosecution, imprisonment and violent attacks from their opponents. Ironically, the same men who proclaimed their chivalry in fighting to protect Australian womanhood from the violence of 'the Hun', were only too willing them selves to assault Australian women. Mary Grant, for instance, was attacked by soldiers when she attempted to address a meeting organised by the No Conscription Fellowship in Melbourne in May 1916. While fist-fights broke out between soldiers and anti-conscriptionist men in the audience, a group of soldiers seized Grant in order to prevent her speaking to the crowd. The *Socialist* newspaper reported that the soldiers 'came like a pack of wolves':

Her coat was torn in a dozen places, her blouse ripped open, her [Labor] badge flung far and wide, and the marks of claws are still upon her arm, where they pinched her to get her away.[3]

Document 4.2

The Women's Peace Army

(Merrifield Collection, Ms 13045, La Trobe Library, Melbourne)

JOIN

The Australian Women's Peace Army

(Affiliated to the International Committee of Women for Permanent Peace).

TOWARDS PERMANENT PEACE.

Equality of Rights and Opportunities for Men and Women of ALL Nations.

Australian Headquarters:
The Guild Hall,
Swanston Street,
Melbourne.

President: Miss VIDA GOLDSTEIN.
Hon. Sec.: Miss CECILIA JOHN.
Organiser: Miss ADELA PANKHURST.

MEMBERSHIP FEE: Voluntary, with Entrance Fee of 1/-

PLATFORM.

1. **Abolition of Conscription** and Every Form of **Militarism.**
2. **Women** to be given Equal Political Rights with Men in all Countries where Representative Government Exists.
3. **Education of Children** in Principles of Anti-Militarism and Internationalism.
4. **Self-Government** Not to be Refused to Any People.
5. **Respect for Nationality.**—No Territory to be Transferred without the consent of the men and women in it. The right of conquest not to be recognised.
6. **Foreign Policy** to be Subject to Democratic Control.
7. **General Disarmament** to be aimed at by the Governments taking over the manufacture of the munitions of war and controlling International traffic in them.
8. **Trade Routes** to be open on equal terms to the shipping of all nations.
9. **Investments** to be made at the risk of the Investor, without claim to the official protection of his Government.
10. **Secret Treaties** to be void, and the theory of the **Balance of Power** to be abandoned.
11. **Our Social System** to be remodelled on a basis of co-operation, so that production and distribution shall be controlled by the people for the people.
12. **International Disputes** to be referred to an International Court of Justice, in which men and women of all classes shall be represented.

JOIN THE WOMEN'S PEACE ARMY NOW!

■ What does the platform of the Australian Women's Peace Army tell us about this group's analysis of the causes of war, and its cures?
■ How does that analysis compare to that offered by Eleanor Moore of the International Sisterhood for Peace (Document 4.3)?

The report went on to describe how even after the main fighting subsided, Grant remained a focus of attack, with soldiers pulling her chair from under her as she attempted to make some notes. They 'threw her on the floor and kicked her... She was then attacked [from behind] by a number of soldiers.'

Two months earlier, Mary, Adela Pankhurst and Vida Goldstein had all been jostled and pushed by soldiers when they attempted to speak against conscription on the Yarra Bank, a

---

Document 4.3

Women urged to vote NO

(Eleanor Moore, *Conscription and Women's Loyalty*, Melbourne, 1917)

Conscription

and **Woman's Loyalty.**

By ELEANOR M. MOORE.

I AM A WOMAN. I can only be loyal in a woman's way. I cannot give to the State what is not mine. Giving away other people's money is not generosity; it is theft. Voting away other people's liberty is not patriotism; it is persecution. Forcing other people to risk their lives for me is not courage; it is cowardice.

I AM A WOMAN. I was given a vote that I might impress my womanly feeling and point of view on public life. If I use that vote to strengthen men's faith in violence and revenge as against intelligence and moral force, my influence is worse than wasted.

I AM A WOMAN. I deny the right of any man or State to force me to produce life against my will. On the same principle, I recognise that I have no right to force any man to take life against his will.

I AM A WOMAN. Australia has given me the rights of citizenship. In return I must do my part to save Australia from becoming a prey to the militarism which has brought Europe to ruin. I see that, but for conscription, the present war would have been impossible. I must keep Australia free from that curse while yet there is time.

I AM A WOMAN. I have an obligation to the men at the Front, but I know I cannot relieve them by swelling the number of sufferers. I believe the glory of man is not in his brute strength and violence, but in his powers of intellect and spirit. For the relief of the agonised youth of all nations, our own included, I demand that he use these powers to bring the present war to an end.

I AM A WOMAN. I know that the idea that lasting peace can be gained by war is nonsense. I know that no war, however victorious, has ever produced lasting peace. I know that a just and honourable peace, such as the people of all belligerent nations are thirsting for and ready for, has a far greater chance of being permanent if arranged by negotiation than if brought about in any other way. I know that, however long the fight continues, in the end it MUST be settled by negotiation.

I AM A WOMAN. I know that everywhere and always, when men make war on men, the sufferings of such as myself are indescribably horrible. I know that as long as war continues such suffering cannot be prevented or mitigated. For this reason I will not sanction the war system by forcing any man to be a soldier.

I AM A WOMAN. For the honour of womanhood, for the glory of Australia, and for the encouragement of men to be true to the highest in them, I mean to record a vote of WANT OF CONFIDENCE IN WAR, and

Vote NO !!!

Fraser and Jenkinson, Print,
143-5 Queen St., Melb

Authorised by T. J. Miller,
Lees Street, Bentleigh.

traditional public speaking forum in Melbourne. The soldiers particularly objected to the women speaking because they believed that women at a previous meeting had referred to soldiers as 'murderers' and 'assassins', a charge the speakers denied. One soldier was reported as saying that 'if the men here did to the women what the Germans have done to Belgium women I would stand by and watch them do it with pleasure'. The other soldiers cheered this threat of rape, then 30 of them set upon one of the men on the platform, who was determined to protect the women, and attempted to throw him in the river.[4] The violence directed against the 'antis' became such a regular feature of the campaigns that an 'Anti Conscription Army' was formed to protect speakers and marchers (of both sexes) against the violence of soldiers.

It was not only soldiers who physically assaulted women peace and anti-conscription activists. At a public meeting held in 1917 by a pro-conscription group, Margaret Thorp, a Queensland Quaker and leader of the Brisbane WPA, was dragged to the floor, 'punched and scratched, rolled on the floor, kicked and punched, and scratched again' by an angry crowd of women as she attempted to speak during the meeting.[5] Pandemonium broke out among the female crowd as the 230-strong conscription supporters battled with the 20 to 30 'antis', slapping faces, pulling hair, tearing clothes and engaging in 'actual fisticuffs'. Thorp's repeated attempts to ascend the platform were met by renewed violence against her and her handful of supporters, culminating in Thorp and two others being physically thrown from the hall.

How can we explain such 'unladylike' behaviour on the part of normally respectable, law-abiding women? The answer probably lies with the intensity of the issues at stake. The women who assaulted the hapless peace activists were venting their anger and grief at what they saw as the unequal way in which they had to bear the burden of the war casualties. Most of the women active in the pro-conscription campaigns had close male relatives —

Document 4.4

A women's 'no-conscription' procession

Documents 4.4 and 4.5 are two accounts of the same event: one appeared in the *Woman Voter*, the official journal of the Women's Political Association and the Australian Women's Peace Army; the other in the Melbourne *Age*, a major daily newspaper supporting conscription. Read both before answering the questions on page 78.

The procession and demonstration by the United Women's No-Conscription Committee was a supreme success. An ideal day, between 4000 and 6000 women processionists where only 2000 had been hoped for, artistic tableaux and singing, a seething, sympathetic mass of onlookers along the route, a concourse of 80,000 people on Yarra Bank, earnest, thoughtful speeches, produced a demonstration of popular feeling such as has never before been witnessed in Australia. There was nothing to mar its success except a few ugly, isolated attempts by a few soldiers of the hooligan type, who find their way into every army, to attack the women and children who took part in the procession.

And the pity of it! So desperate is the Press in its effort to fasten Conscription on Australia that mendacity and malice of the most venomous kind were employed to make those who could not see the proceedings believe that violence and rioting were the chief features. The meanest and most cowardly weapon was used by the *Age*, which concluded its account by saying: 'It was significant that, following in the rear of the procession were men engaged in selling *Direct Action*, the official organ of the I.W.W. [Industrial Workers of the World].'

The procession, which started from the Guild Hall at the appointed time, was headed by Madge Gardiner, 8 years of age, the youngest daughter of Mrs. Gardiner, vice-president of the W.P.A., dressed in white, and carrying the dove of peace; behind her two young girls carried a banner, which bore the words: 'A Little Child Shall Lead Them'. Then followed the Chief Marshal, Miss Cecilia John, in white, carrying a staff, with a very handsome decoration in the colours of the Women's Peace Army — purple, white and green. Next in order came the United Women's No-Conscription Committee, in fours, headed by Mrs. Wallace and Miss Goldstein (presidents), Mrs. Bremner and Miss Moody (secretaries), Miss Adela Pankhurst, Mrs. Singleton, Mrs. Killury, Miss Lewis, Miss Fullerton, etc.; eight lorries, with tableaux representing 'Free Australia', 'Happy Childhood', 'War and Peace', 'Peace', 'Food Exploiters', 'International', 'No', 'White Australia', banners and sandwich boards inscribed with 'Thou Shalt Not Kill', 'Brotherhood', 'Sisterhood', 'Liberty of Conscience', 'Women of the World, Unite', 'The Prime Minister's Light is Australia's Darkness', 'We Follow Our Light', 'We Are Awake', 'It is Easier to Make Chains Than to Break Them', 'Our Sons are Our Own', 'Lost, A Democrat, For Sale (Cheap), An Autocrat', and many others. Processionists carried 'No' and 'Australia' standards, coloured blue and white (Labour), red (Socialist), and purple, white and green (W.P.A.). The women of Wonthaggi were specially represented with a banner, 'Wonthaggi Women Say "No"'. Individual supporters came from distant country towns to take part in the demonstration. Motor cars and vehicles were provided for hoary-headed but free-souled women who were unable to walk. The children on lorries won the hearts of many, one old man remarking, 'I was going to vote "Yes", but when I look at those children I see I must vote "No".'

Miss Boquest, as marshal, on a grey horse, kept the line in order, and at a given signal several dozen peace doves were liberated from the children's lorries.

As the procession reached Bourke Street, an attempt was made by about 30 soldiers to disorganise the procession, but Mr. F. J. Riley had gathered a group of as many men supporters, and the soldiers were quickly pushed back. One of the men picked up our little herald of peace to protect her from the soldiers, and she remained mounted on his shoulder, with her white dove held aloft. Other attempts were made by knots of soldiers to interfere with the procession, but other soldiers linked arms and prevented them effecting their purpose. It was noticeable that many of the returned soldiers along the route heartily cheered the processionists. Individual soldiers here and there attacked the women and children, snatching their 'No' standards from them and breaking them in their faces; one soldier bit off a piece of the finger of a woman who resisted his savagery. Again, at the Yarra Bank, a few soldiers appeared on the outskirts of the crowd and endeavoured to create a disturbance, but they were soon escorted from the ground by the police. At no time did any of the soldiers gain control of the situation, and not one speaker was interrupted by soldiers. A soldier spoke against Conscription from the 'Peace' platform of the W.P.A. It was reported in the Press that a number of young girls sang a 'hymn of hate', with the refrain, 'We hate you, Billy Hughes'. If so, it was not official, and was merely the good-humoured answer of enthusiastic girls to the hymn of love sung in Mr. Hughes' ears by English duchesses.

The speakers were Mrs. Wallace, Miss Goldstein, Miss Adela Pankhurst, Mrs. Hickey, Mrs. Baines, Mrs. Webb, Mrs. Singleton, Misses [sic] Grant, Miss Fullerton, Mrs. Foster, Miss Lewis and Miss Daley, whose speeches were received with the greatest enthusiasm.

* * *

The above account of an epoch-making event in Australian history is true in every particular, and stands out in sharp contrast to the malicious reports in the daily papers.

(*Woman Voter*, 28 October 1916)

Anti-conscription: Women's demonstration

Scenes in the city: Acts of violence

Wild scenes of disorder and violence attended a women's anti-conscription demonstration in the city on Saturday afternoon. Attracted by two processions — one in connection with the Police carnival at the Exhibition Building, and the other the parade of women promoted by the United Women's No-Conscription Committee — an immense crowd of about 60,000 people gathered in Swanston Street, between the Guild Hall and Princes Bridge, and for upwards of an hour the street was a surging sea of humanity. The excitement was intense while the two processions, marching in opposite directions, forced their way through the great mass of people to the strains of bands, the screams of women and children, and scenes of the utmost disorder. The processions came into conflict with one another at the intersection of Bourke and Swanston…and…feeling ran so high between the conscriptionists and anti-conscriptionists that acts of violence were repeatedly resorted to.

Walking at the head of the women's procession was a little girl in white, bearing aloft a dove, and a bannerette which followed bore the motto 'And a little child shall lead them.' Several constables had the greatest difficulty in clearing a passage, and, after going a few paces, the child was caught up by a man of sturdy build and carried the rest of the way. Whilst the procession was stationary on the north side of Bourke Street several men rushed one of the lorries bearing a tableau, and, amid the screaming of women and children, swept away a number of 'Vote No' devices which were carried by the children. Shortly afterwards a group of men bore down on several women who were carrying a bannerette, and endeavoured to snatch it away from them. Mrs J. Riley, a member of the Socialist party, ran to their assistance, and was somewhat severely handled. To the inspiring strains of the 'Marseillaise', 'Australia Will Be There' and other selections, and the accompaniment of singing by the women and children, including a hymn of hate, winding up with the words 'We hate you, Billy Hughes', the procession continued on its way to the Yarra bank. Mr Maloney, M.P., was the only member of Parliament present at the proceedings, and he took a prominent part in endeavouring to maintain order and protect the women and children. On arrival at the Yarra bank the lorries bearing the various tableaus were drawn up in various parts of the reserve, and the concourse of people which had gathered, estimated to number between 20,000 and 30,000, assembled around them to listen to speeches on anti-conscription from the members of the no-conscription committee.

Shortly afterwards a cry went up that the soldiers were coming, and there was a stampede of men towards the south-east portion of the reserve, where a squad of about 30 soldiers was seen to be marching towards the main crowd. The soldiers were accompanied by one of their crippled comrades in a bath chair, which was a strong indication that they had no intention of breaking up the meeting, but merely wished to show by their presence that they were opposed to the anti-conscriptionists. However that may be, the cry was quickly raised, 'Protect the women and children', and a scene of the most riotous character ensued. Urged to frenzy by the mere contemplation of violence to the women and children, the men got out of all bounds and made savage attacks on the soldiers, who were compelled to act on the defensive. It was almost tragic to see the small number of men in khaki surrounded by a howling mob of about 500 men, eager to tear them to pieces or to throw them into the Yarra… Gradually the soldiers gave way, and there was a great outburst of cheering when they eventually left the enclosed area and mingled among the crowd on the roadway…

When the procession was passing the Town Hall several stale eggs were thrown at the processionists… It was significant that, following in the rear of the procession, were men engaged in selling 'Direct Action', the official organ of the I.W.W. [Industrial Workers of the World].

(*Age*, 23 October 1916)

■ How do the two accounts (Documents 4.4 and 4.5) differ? Is it possible to decide which is more accurate?
■ Which account would have had more influence on public perceptions of the procession?

husbands and sons — fighting at the Front. Mrs Anna E. Paterson, the main organiser of this particular meeting, for instance, had a husband doing essential war work as a munitions engineer in England, and three sons fighting in France. Mrs Josey Reid, secretary of the organisation, claimed that 'the majority' of those present were 'mourning the loss of some dear one who has either gone down in the conflict or will only come back to them maimed or impaired'.[6] She and her associates had formed the Women's Compulsory Service Petition League, hoping to secure the signatures of 20 000 Queensland women on a petition urging the Prime Minister to introduce conscription without another referendum. The eruption into an unprecedented expression of fury arguably owes something to the deep grief and anxiety felt by many of these women. Such grief was probably made harder to bear because of the wartime insistence that relatives accept their loss bravely and without fuss, 'for the Empire's sake'. And as the war progressed, the numbers directly affected by the horrendous casualty lists had grown and grown. To have women such as Thorp deny the necessity of the war itself and the massive sacrifices it entailed was simply too much for many women (and men) to bear and they lashed out in a way that would have been unthinkable in normal times.

However, physical assaults were not condoned by all the conscriptionists present (Mrs McLennan, who moved the original motion, declared her disgust at the disturbance which she characterised as 'rampant emotionalism'[7]). Nor was it the most usual tactic employed by women supporting the war. As we have seen, patriotic women spent vast amounts of energy organising 'comforts' for the fighting men. Well before the conscription campaigns of 1916 and 1917, they had engaged in a concerted propaganda campaign, designed to encourage, shame and blackmail reluctant men into enlisting. Determined young women beckoned passers by into recruitment booths, urging them to prove their manhood and do their bit for Empire. And women were at the centre of many government-sponsored recruitment meetings. Those unconvinced by the stories of returned and wounded soldiers would sometimes succumb to the vocal persuasion of women like Miss Madge Jacklyn. In 1915, she sang 'We don't want to lose you, but we think you ought to go' to audiences of several hundred in the towns of Tasmania.

The most spectacular enlistment drives were initiated as the disastrous campaign in the Dardanelles took its grim toll on the original Anzacs. Recruitment marchers set out, young men trekking hundreds of miles through country districts to the city. The Coo-ees began in Gilgandra with 30 men; by the time they reached Sydney, 200 more had joined them. They were followed by the Waratahs (from Nowra), the Kangaroos (from Wagga Wagga) and the Wallabies (from Narrabri).

■ Read Document 4.6. What reasons does 'Jim Bluegum' give for enlisting, and what do these tell us about his social background?

■ Why was Jean so important a consideration?

■ Do you think this letter is genuine? Why? If not, why would it have been published in a volume of love letters in 1916?

While it was men who marched, they would not have got far without the support of women. Patriotic leagues and individual housewives provided meals and entertainments along the way, and for many a mile the marchers were cheered on by escorts of women and children. The impromptu recruitment meetings held at towns en route emphasised once again women's part in the enlistment effort. As the Coo-ees neared Redfern, Mrs Annie Hunter clambered onto a makeshift recruitment platform. 'I had only three boys', she declared, 'and two have been killed; the third one is with the Coo-ees, and I wish I had another to give in the cause of Empire.'

This kind of appeal to men's sense of shame was arguably the most powerful weapon in the patriotic women's rhetoric. From the early years of the war, 'white feather' leagues were established throughout Australia. Members forwarded a white feather to selected men of eligible age, along with the simple message: COWARD. Even schoolgirls joined in. A member of IIID English class at Sydney Girls High School called on Australia's sons 'to help the Motherland':

And so to-day they're fighting,
    And dying o'er the foam,
While you, ye laggards, linger
    Here in your sunny home.

And there on France's acres
    The great world-fight is fought,
Where all men live as brothers,
    Or die as brave men ought.

And here at home the women,
    With breaking hearts, yet true,
Are working, waiting, hoping,
    For those who die for *you*![8]

The pro-conscription campaigns can be seen as a continuation of earlier recruiting efforts, resorting to compulsion where voluntarism had failed. The leaders of the women's pro-conscription campaigns tended to be of the same type as those prominent in the White Feather League: middle-class women with strong connections to conservative political groups. They believed implicitly in the righteousness of the imperial cause and the justice of temporarily denying individual liberties for the sake of this 'greater' cause.

Women not only organised and spoke at conscription meetings, but were also the targets of much of the propaganda generated by both sides during the campaigns. The First World War is noted for the extremism in the general propaganda produced. As the first 'total war', involving civilians as well as soldiers in an unprecedented way, it was a war for the hearts and minds of the people as well as for front line military advantage. Armed with new printing techniques, wartime propagandists showed no restraint. They created sensational posters and pamphlets which

Document 4.6

Jim Bluegum

Sydney, September 17, 1914

My dearest Jean,

I've got news for you, Honeybunch: startling news potent with grave possibilities for us both. It's the biggest item of news which any young man can, in these stirring days, tell to his sweetheart. Aye, your own heart will have told you. *I'm a soldier of the King!* I write it proudly: I could do nothing other than enlist.

This is going to be a big war, a long war, the greatest war this old world has ever seen. Within a year the streets of Sydney will be placarded with big posters, 'Your Country needs *you*.' I don't want to go to war as the result of the importunity of Kitchener. I don't want my friends to point their fingers at me and say, 'Why don't *you* go?' Most of all, darling, I don't want *you* to lift your lovely blue eyes to mine, wondering if I will play the man. I want you to feel and know that when the Empire called, *your* MAN answered.

I fought it all out the other night, Honey. I weighed the pros and cons so judiciously. I reminded myself that I was thirty-four years of age, and that it was right and proper for all the younger men to go first. I looked round my library at all my books and thought of the bitterness of parting... I let my hand rest lovingly on some old pocket editions that had shared with me many a ramble... I smoked another cigar and remembered with a kind of shudder that cigars are not always procurable on active service.

Then, with a rush, came thoughts of the rigours and horrors of war: cold, sleepless nights; long weary marches; hot, thirsty days; fierce, bloody battle; maybe wounds and death. *Death!* Fancy dying with so little done and so much to do! I had given so little to the world in return for all the good things showered on me. I had done so little for Old England in return for my priceless British Citizenship. And sunny Australia — land of my birth: year after year I had roamed her fertile fields, sailed her tropic seas and climbed her rugged mountains. How little had I given in return! How trivial my services towards the making of the nation...

I thought the whole thing out, dearest one. I fought the whole thing out, and I felt I could go out to battle for Empire, leaving behind home and friends... But I was not quite sure, my darling, if I could leave *you*. Then I looked up at the wall and saw your picture — the one I love. Near by — curiously apposite — was the picture of

His Majesty, King George V. Somehow the final tussle resolved itself into King or Love... I stood irresolute, gazing first on one picture, then on the other...

For a brief space I thought I'd toss for it; I even took a coin from my pocket. Then I scouted that idea as silly and cowardly: I alone had to make my decision; I could not trust it to the spin of a coin.

I took your picture down from the wall and gazed at it, oh, so fondly... There could be only one answer... You always were my inspiration... And I could have sworn the picture smiled approval when I made the great decision. You know it was not that I loved thee less, but Empire more. 'I could not leave thee, dear, so well, loved I not honour more.' I'd often heard that, but never knew what it meant till now. God bless you, my own.

I went up to the barracks in the morning. The rush was, is, still on. Since the Prime Minister offered 20,000 men for the service of the Empire, there has been a great rush of patriotic volunteers. It would have gladdened Kitchener's heart to see them. I went straight to the Commandant, and he was awfully nice. I can't write down all the kind things he said. Major Irvine asked me to come along to the 1st Australian Infantry Brigade, and he would try and get me a commission [officer's rank]. I thanked him, but said I had decided for the Light Horse. Then I went round to the mounted men. But the officers had all been selected, and there were hundreds more mounted men — sun-tanned bushmen from all parts of sunny New South Wales — offering than were needed. Also I heard that there were over a hundred applicants for commissions in the next Light Horse regiment. I was terribly disappointed, sweetheart, but there seemed only one thing to do and I did it. I went straight out to camp at Rosebery Park and enlisted as a trooper...

We can't leave for the Front for some time yet, my sweet one. But come down to town as soon as you can. I'm longing to see you. I know you'll be brave, full of smiles and commendations. But hurry. Think of all the long and weary months we must spend apart. Now that I'm a soldier of the King I can get only a few hours' leave. Otherwise I'd take the first train for Erringhi. Wire when you're coming...

Till we meet, Heart of my Heart,
Your soldier,
Jim Bluegum

(Oliver Hogue, *Love Letters of an Anzac*, London, 1916, pp. 9–13. First published February 1916; reprinted in March and November 1916.)

appealed directly to popular emotions, engendering deep hatred for the enemy abroad and for real or imagined enemies at home. In Britain, images of raped Belgian and French women (appealing to men's chivalry and women's fears) were used to gain support for the war effort. In Australia, the fact that women had the vote made them clearer targets for the propagandists of both sides, especially during the conscription campaigns.

Propaganda targeted at women was different from that directed at men because conscription had different implications for women. Although women could now vote, they were not the ones eligible for conscription — their role as citizens in wartime was to *produce* warriors, not *be* warriors. It was commonly believed that women were more susceptible than men to emotional appeals to their nurturing qualities. Because women gave birth, breast-fed and reared children, they were less likely, it was felt, to support a measure which would inevitably mean the deaths of their own children or those of other mothers. The messages directed at women also had a heavy component of guilt, asking women how they could in all conscience send men to their deaths when they themselves would be safe at home. Thus, Vida Goldstein, in a 'Special Appeal by Women to Women', argued that women, along with men, had a duty to protect Australia from the militarism of society which would inevitably come with conscription. But, she insisted, women had a 'greater responsibility in this matter than men'.

■ Why do you think the authorities found this song so threatening to recruitment that they banned it?
■ What does their action suggest about the role of women in the war effort?

Document 4.7

'I Didn't Raise My Son To Be A Soldier'

Once when a mother was asked would she send
   Her darling boy to fight,
She just answered 'No'
   And I think you'll admit she was right.

CHORUS
I didn't raise my son to be a soldier,
   I brought him up to be my pride and joy;
Who dares to put a musket on his shoulder
   To kill some other mother's darling boy?

The nations ought to arbitrate their quarrels.
   It's time to put the sword and gun away,
There'd be no war to-day if mothers all would say;
   I didn't raise my son to be a soldier.

All men are brothers, our country, the world;
   The glories of war are a lie;
If they ask us why
   We'll just tell them that mother's reply...

('Women's Anti-Conscription Songs', Ms 2123, La Trobe Library, Melbourne)

As the Mothers of the Race, it is your privilege to conserve life, and love, and beauty, all of which are destroyed by war. Without them, the world is a desert.

You, who give life, cannot, if you think deeply and without bias, vote to send any mother's son to kill, against his will, some other mother's son.

You may, if you choose, send your own son, but you are guilty in the first degree if you take upon yourself the responsibility of forcing someone else's son to break the Sixth Commandment, and, defying God, say to him: THOU SHALT KILL.[9]

These sentiments were expressed even more forcefully in posters such as 'The Blood Vote' and 'The Mothers' (see Documents 4.12 and 4.14). The conscriptionists responded to this appeal to women's 'natural' passivity by arguing that they would indirectly be preserving lives by sending reinforcements to the men already fighting. However, the connections between compulsory military service and the preservation of life were not easy to sustain, so conscription propaganda tended to appeal to a wider range of human emotion and to rely less on evoking women's 'natural' purity and nurturing qualities (see Documents 4.7 to 4.20).

■ Read document 4.8. What is the 'pro' answer to the fear about cheap imported labour?
■ Would workers have been reassured by the suggestion (see Document 4.9) that Australian *women* could take the place of men in the workplace? Why?

Document 4.8

Women urged to vote YES

One anti-conscription argument was that conscription of Australian men would reduce the standard of living of working-class people because (cheaper) foreign workers would have to be imported. This document is a response to that argument. (Ms 3637, La Trobe Library, Melbourne)

WOMEN OF AUSTRALIA!.

Be not misled by the blatant lie—that if the Referendum is carried Australia will be flooded with cheap coloured labour.

The carrying of the Referendum in no way affects our Alien Restriction Act. Ask yourselves:—What has enabled Australia—an island continent in the Southern Seas—to establish and maintain her White Australia Policy Is it not the fact that we are part of the British Empire, protected by the British Fleet ? Is it not also a fact that so long as we enjoy the protection of the British Fleet we can by the power of the vote prevent any change in our national policy ? Are WE, the Women of Australia, not as well able to work for our dear land as the Women of Britain and France ? If we stand shoulder to shoulder with Britain and her Allies to the bitter end—as we should do—do you think that Britain would be a party to the crushing of one of the most cherished ideals of the land that bred the Anzac ? NEVER !

Vote "YES"
AND NAIL THE COLOURED LIE.

For the Women's Committee of the National Campaign for Compulsory Reinforcements.

Joint Hon. Secs. { ELEANOR MacKINNON, { Dalton House, Pitt Street, { GRACE L. SCOBIE, { Sydney.

Authorised by Hector Lamond and F. J. Thomas, 115 Pitt St., Sydney.

William Brooks & Co., Ltd., Printers. Sydney.

Document 4.9

Women as farm labourers

(*Worker* [Brisbane], 20 December 1917)

Australia's Pioneer Co-operative Labor Journal.

Vol. 28—No. 1390.   BRISBANE, THURSDAY, DECEMBER 20, 1917.   Price, One Penny.

WHAT WILL HAPPEN TO WOMEN.
DOES AUSTRALIA STAND FOR THIS?

The following is a passage taken from a report published in the Brisbane "Courier" of December 5 of a meeting addressed by Prime Minister Hughes in Sydney on the previous day:

"REPLYING TO A QUESTION, MR. HUGHES STATED THAT HE INTENDED TO ORGANISE THE WOMEN OF AUSTRALIA ALONG THE LINES OF THE ORGANISATION OF THE WOMEN OF FRANCE AND ENGLAND, WITH A VIEW TO FREEING MEN FOR ACTIVE SERVICE."

The "New York Times" of August 12 last reproduces the above photograph of women of France working in the fields as "farm horses." Beneath the photograph is the following:

"WHILE THE MEN AND HORSES OF FRANCE FIGHT HER BATTLES AT THE FRONT, HER WOMEN ARE TAKING THE PLACES OF BOTH IN THE FIELDS AT HOME."

PEOPLE OF QUEENSLAND, do you stand for making farm horses of your women while the profiteers and capitalists, with their bejewelled dames and pampered daughters, wallow in the luxury of their ill-gotten gains? If not,

"Vote NO."
KEEP AUSTRALIA FREE.

J. S. Butlin, 164 Elizabeth Street, Brisbane.

Document 4.10

Why a woman should vote YES

(Ms 3200, La Trobe Library, Melbourne)

No. 20

Why a Woman Should Vote YES.

BECAUSE

1. Her son and other women's sons in the trenches are begging for relief and rest.

BECAUSE

2. He is on duty day after day, contending with mud, cold, want of sleep, appalling sights and sounds, home-sickness, war-weariness. Will you not send him help?

BECAUSE

3. Although human life is sacred, justice and liberty are more sacred still, and all through history brave men have been ready and willing to risk their lives for a noble cause. You would not like to think Australians preferred their skins to their duty.

BECAUSE

4. You know all this outcry about producing food being preferable to sending reinforcements is a mere party cry—and that the Government will keep enough men in the country to carry on the necessary industries.

BECAUSE

5. Safety of Australia is intimately bound up with the safety of the Empire. If the Allies fall, Australia falls, and Australians will become German slaves, and the women will be treated as Belgian and French women have been treated.

BECAUSE

6. A very small reinforcement has often changed defeat into victory. The battle of the Marne was won and the course of history changed by a single Division. Think how proud you would be if our five Divisions proved the turning point in this War?

YES.

Authorised by Percy Hunter, Chief Organiser, and Archdale Parkhill, General Secretary, Reinforcements Referendum Council, Sydney.

William Brooks & Co., Ltd., Printers, 17 Castlereagh Street, Sydney,

■ Identify the different emotional appeals being made in Documents 4.10 and 4.11. Is there any difference between them?

Document 4.11

Why girls should vote YES

(Ms 3200, La Trobe Library, Melbourne)

No. 21a

Why Girls Should Vote YES

Because

A Girl would be ashamed to know her countrymen had not taken their full share in the war.

Because

She would not like to think that Australians are inferior to the French, English, Americans, and others who are sending their sons to the Front.

Because

She hated last year to hear men say the Russians will do the job. And she hates now to hear them say "The Americans will do the job." She wants Australians to do their own job.

Because

She is sick of hearing all these recruiting appeals producing so little result. She feels ashamed of the male species, and wishes she was a man.

Because

She is disgusted to see certain men only thinking of amusing themselves frequenting Racecourses, the Stadium, and other pleasure resorts, while other men are bleeding on the battlefield.

Because

She thinks that many of the "Shirkers" are not cowards, but that they simply don't realise the awful danger of to-day, and fail to understand that Australia is in actual peril.

Because

She knows what other girls are suffering and what her own fate may be if Germans conquer Australia, and, therefore, she means not only to vote herself, but to entreat every other Girl to vote

YES

Authorised by Percy Hunter, General Organiser, and Archdale Parkhill, General Secretary, Reinforcements Referendum Council, Sydney

The H. H. Watson Printing Co., Druitt and Kent Streets, Sydney.

The Blood Vote

(Ms 3200, La Trobe Library, Melbourne)

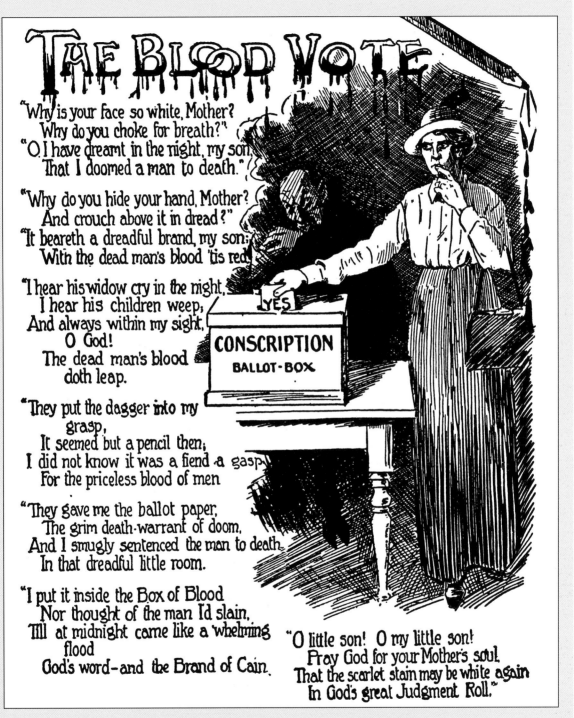

THE BLOOD VOTE

"Why is your face so white, Mother?
  Why do you choke for breath?"
"O I have dreamt in the night, my son,
  That I doomed a man to death."

"Why do you hide your hand, Mother?
  And crouch above it in dread?"
"It beareth a dreadful brand, my son;
  With the dead man's blood 'tis red."

"I hear his widow cry in the night,
  I hear his children weep;
And always within my sight,
    O God!
  The dead man's blood
    doth leap.

"They put the dagger into my
    grasp,
  It seemed but a pencil then;
I did not know it was a fiend a gasp,
  For the priceless blood of men

"They gave me the ballot paper,
  The grim death-warrant of doom,
And I smugly sentenced the man to death
  In that dreadful little room.

"I put it inside the Box of Blood
  Nor thought of the man I'd slain,
Till at midnight came like a whelming
    flood
  God's word—and the Brand of Cain.

"O little son! O my little son!
  Pray God for your Mother's soul,
That the scarlet stain may be white again
  In God's great Judgment Roll."

CONSCRIPTION BALLOT-BOX

YES

■ Compare the special appeals to women in Documents 4.12 and
4.13. What is the moral issue in each case? How does each
propagandist suggest that the voter resolve this moral issue?

Document 4.13

The sanctity of human life

ANTI-PERSON: Don't worry, don't worry, my woman! You'll be all right. Tell him that human life is sacred!
(Ms 3200, La Trobe Library, Melbourne)

■ What message is the cartoon above conveying about the personal qualities and principles of those opposed to conscription? How is this message conveyed? Who is it likely to appeal to?

■ Documents 4.14, 4.15 and 4.16 appeal to women as mothers in an attempt to influence their attitude to enlistment. What conclusions does each expect 'mothers' to reach?

Document 4.14

God bless dear Daddy...

(Australian Government, poster illustrated by Norman Lindsay)

Document 4.15

The Mothers

(Ms 3200, La Trobe Library, Melbourne)

- The article below appears to be addressed to all women, but is it more likely to appeal to certain classes of women than others?
- Is it likely to appeal to the same women as might be impressed by the propaganda of Document 4.18?

Document 4.16

'Mother, how did you vote on the Great Referendum?'

THE WIDOW: I relied on Mr. Hughes's promise that married men would not be needed and voted 'yes'.
(Ms 13045, La Trobe Library, Melbourne)

Document 4.17

Women and conscription

(Merrifield Collection, Ms 13045, La Trobe Library)

WOMEN AND CONSCRIPTION

("Australian Worker," Oct. 5.)

Women do not love war.

War has always smitten women more heavily than men.

It takes away woman's chief source of livelihood; destroys the lives of both her strong men and her babies; and degrades her womanhood more than any other evil thing has power to do.

In military-controlled countries the women are bearers of children and beasts of burden only.

In military-controlled countries force is the highest ideal, and the battle being always to the strong, the women and children, as the weakest in the nation, suffer most.

War makes food scarce, and in the fighting countries of Europe to-day for every soldier that has been killed in battle eight babies have died for want of proper nourishment.

War makes labour cheap. As the strongest, healthiest men are taken to glut the God of Battles, the weak and the feeble, and the helpless, old, and young are forced to carry on the ordinary work of profit-making at whatever wage the profit-mongers care to pay them.

Under Conscription in France to-day women are working 12 hours a day for 14s. per week on work which, before the war, men got 28s. per week for performing. The difference of 14s. per week does not go into the revenue of France, to help pay the cost of war, but into the pocket of the private employer. There is no hope of any successful protest from the workers of France, either against this wholesale lowering of the standard of wages, nor against the importation of Chinese or African workers, because the workers are under military control.

Under Conscription in Great Britain women are working in munition making and other "war" trades at 13s. 11d. per week of 60 hours, and if these women leave their work without the permission of the employers the penalty for other people employing them is anything between £50 and £100.

Postwomen in England are working for 7s. 6d. per week. Farm labourers (and 45 per cent. of the farm labourers are women) are getting 7s. 6d. per week. Up to June last there were 300,000 children under the school age (14 years) working for a maximum rate of 7s. 6d. per week.

When women in Australia read glowing accounts of the magnificent arrangements for munition workers in the United Kingdom to-day, they should remember that, in scores of places, workers have been so crowded together that three women shared the same bed in relays of eight-hour shifts. Huge tenement houses have been erected (and rushed for occupancy by workers), and advertised as "one-room homes for workers," where, for 6s. 6d. or 7s. 6d. per week, you could have a home, with your stove on one side of the room, your bed on the other, and your sitting-room in the middle of the 12ft. x 12ft. compartment.

Do Australian women want to have these conditions here?

Australian boys and men have offered themselves 300,000 strong to go forth and fight against the evils of Conscription in other lands—WILL THE WOMEN HERE BE SO BLIND AS TO ASSIST IN FASTENING CONSCRIPTION UPON THEIR OWN DEAR LAND WHILE THEY ARE AWAY?

For women have only the promise of perjured politicians that this monster is to live on them "for the term of the war" only.

WOMEN OF AUSTRALIA, as your men have gone—so they believed—to crush militarism, and to protect you from its ravages, see that you prove yourselves worthy mates of the men of Gallipoli by protecting yourselves and your children from the same foe within your gates.

Be not deceived by specious pleading. War is war, and military control crushes every semblance of freedom for the working people by whatever power it may be imposed.

—Jennie Scott Griffiths, St. Andrew's Place, Sydney.

Document 4.18

The new 'bullocky'

(Merrifield Collection, Ms 13045, La Trobe Library, Melbourne)

Document 4.19

Biddy: I sez NO!

(*Comment and Cartoons*, 7 December 1917, p. 9, Ferguson Collection, National Library of Australia)

■ As well as being the *targets* of propaganda, women were also used in propaganda as *symbols*. What is the woman symbolising here and in Document 4.20?

■ Why have the cartoonists chosen these particular types of womanhood to represent the relevant interests?

Document 4.20

'The Only Way'

(*Comments and Cartoons*, 7 December 1917, p. 8, Ferguson Collection, National Library of Australia)

Not all the appeals made to women relied on obvious emotional manipulation. Another 'Appeal to Women', this time in the *Bi-Weekly No!* published by the Anti-Compulsory Service League, insisted that the conscription issue was 'not a matter of sentiment'. Rather, it called upon the 'common sense' of Australian women, pointing out that Australia had already given more men, proportionately, than any other part of the Empire and could not afford to give more. And they did not need to when their more populous allies, especially the United States of America (which had only recently entered the war) could supply all that were required.[10]

Nor did the messages directed to women appeal to them only as females of the species, whose common capacity for mother-hood was their most distinguishing feature. Annie Golding, for instance, a Sydney feminist and labour activist, addressed her 'eloquent appeal' to women as members of the working class. She pointed out that middle-class men and women dominated the pro-conscription campaigns, suggesting that they would be able to find loopholes to keep their own (less numerous) sons out of the trenches while they 'take good care the average workingman will not shelter behind his wife's skirts or his numerous offspring'. Women who advocated conscription and condemned the idleness and simple pleasures of workers, Golding alleged, were social 'butterflies...flaunting their [bright] and expensive attire' at expensive social and sporting events while their husbands whiled away their time in expensive clubs and cafes. Such women, she continued, had no sympathy for the ordinary woman and her 'little ones'.[11]

How effective was all this persuasion directed at Australia's women voters? It is impossible to know, since the referendum figures are not distinguishable by sex. The final votes were very close: a number of contemporary commentators certainly believed that dramatic 'anti' pamphlets such as 'The Blood Vote' swung the votes of a crucial number of women against conscription. Mrs May Holman, wife of the conscriptionist Premier of New South Wales, believed that it was the young women's vote which was crucial: 'They think they will be driving away possible husbands', she explained.[12] But no one really knows if more women than men voted against conscription, nor, if they did, if it was the emotional appeals to their 'natural instincts' that persuaded them rather than their assessments of the general arguments directed at both sexes. What is more certain is the contribution that women made to the organisation and success of the anti-conscription campaigns.

Industrial struggle

Many of the women who campaigned against conscription also found themselves caught up in the industrial upheaval which occurred between the two conscription referendums, from July to October 1917.

The trouble began in Sydney when the government attempted to introduce a new method of work into its railway workshops. Believing that this new system was based on contemporary American methods designed to speed up workers and reduce their control over their work, workers opposed the scheme. The Railway Commissioners and the government refused to negotiate with the men who in August went out on strike. The railway workers were quickly joined by other unionists — mostly in New South Wales but also in Victoria and Queensland — who saw the government's move as yet another attack on workers under the cover of wartime necessity. The situation was further inflamed by the government's allegations that the strike was provoked by pro-German elements. It launched a particularly severe attack on the Industrial Workers of the World (known as the IWW or 'the Wobblies') who were outspoken opponents of the war. By October, the dispute involved almost 100 000 workers who, together, lost four million working days. Other workers were affected when fuel shortages cut power supplies to their particular industries and their homes.

The event became much more than a strike: it was the occasion of huge popular demonstrations against the government of the day and became enmeshed in the politics of wartime. Strikers were attacked as shirkers and pro-German traitors, undermining the war effort from within, while the strikers likened the methods of the Railway Commissioner to those of the Kaiser. The industrial struggle quickly merged into the political one and, as with the battle over conscription, women participated in the public action as well as playing their more traditional supportive roles in strike relief.

From 7 August 1917, the day after the coalminers joined the strike, processions, demonstrations and public mass meetings began to occur on a daily basis, initially in Sydney but in other centres as well as the strike spread. These were spontaneous at first but quickly became well organised and systematic. Prominent unionists and politicians addressed the crowds, depicting the dispute as a struggle between slavery and liberty. They asked in vain for the government to withdraw the card system and appoint an independent arbiter.

Figure 4.2

Strikers' wives marching from the Domain to Parliament House (Sydney)
(*Sydney Mail*, 15 August 1917)

■ **Why did so many women take their babies with them?**

Women were involved in these demonstrations from early in their history. On 9 August, several hundred women led a procession to Parliament House in Sydney where they interviewed the Acting Premier, Mr Fuller, claiming to represent 'fifteen thousand wives of the men on strike as well as women who had entered the industrial field to earn their own living'.[13] The government was unmoved by their requests for an independent tribunal. Instead, it became even more coercive in its approach to the strikers, arresting large numbers of their leaders and rushing through legislation to allow volunteer labour into the coal mines. The government seemed intent on smashing the union movement, which responded with more and bigger demonstrations of protest.

In Sydney on 19 August a crowd of between 80 000 and 150 000 (estimates varied) gathered to protest the government's action and called again for an independent tribunal to settle the dispute. Rather than curbing the strike, the government's attitude encouraged it to spread to an increasing number of occupations and industries throughout the state. As the situation became more serious, the protests became increasingly violent. Volunteers were issued with weapons, which in turn contributed to an escalation of the violence: one striker was killed by a volunteer. Mass demonstrations continued throughout August, including a march of over 100 000 from Wollongong to Sydney. The demonstrations continued even after the strike leaders had negotiated a return to work, as many of the workers felt they had been 'sold out' by the officials. Women continued to be active in these demonstrations, with speakers such as Mrs Jessie Lorimer urging men and women to continue their protests.

Figure 4.3

Sydney women volunteer their services as strike-breakers
(*Sydney Mail*, 29 August, 1917)

■ What social class were these women likely to belong to? Why?

Figure 4.4

With railway workers on strike, women volunteer drivers offered alternative transport.
(*Sydney Mail*, 15 August 1917)

■ How did strike-breaking challenge class and gender roles for women?

Women were involved in these protests as members of the working class, joining with men in a common class struggle. They were present both as strikers and as wives of strikers, seeing an attack on male unionists as affecting all workers, paid and unpaid, regardless of sex. Their presence in the public arena was not a product of the war: working-class women had been fighting the class war in similar ways since the great strikes of the 1890s. What was distinctive about the so-called General Strike of 1917 was the unprecedented scale of the popular protest.

Melbourne food riots

While Sydney was being disrupted by the huge demonstrations of strikers and their supporters, Melbourne (then the nation's capital) was engulfed in a series of dramatic 'food riots'. At the height of these disturbances in late August 1917, a crowd of between five and six thousand people gathered in the Treasury Gardens (next to Parliament House) and were addressed by three women — Adela Pankhurst, Jennie Baines and Alice Suter. Pankhurst urged the crowd to follow her: 'We will defy the police, break into Parliament House if necessary, and see Billy Hughes to know what he will do to give food for the starving children.'[14] The three women, with arms linked, led the crowd towards Parliament House but they were arrested and the crowd dispersed.

A few days later, released on bail, Pankhurst told a Socialist Party meeting:

The high prices caused the recent demonstrations. Parliament will do nothing and it is left to ourselves. We have only one course open and that is to demonstrate. I am not afraid to fight even if it does come to the destruction of property.[15]

Figure 4.5
Adela Pankhurst being arrested
(*Sydney Mail*, 29 August 1917)

■ How did activists like Pankhurst challenge traditional gender roles?

Later that night, a crowd waving red flags marched on Parliament House and windows were smashed in the city streets. The violence increased in the following weeks as demonstrations frequently ended in fights between baton-wielding troopers and demonstrators hurling rocks. The riots ended only after the government formed patrols of special constables to police the city and nearby suburbs.

Women participated in the cost-of-living demonstrations in ways which drew specifically on their particular roles within the family, as well as on their membership of the working class. Melburnians were enduring the bleakest winter of the war. Fourteen and a half thousand men and women were without work for up to two months because of the strike; even those in work could not heat their homes because of a shortage of coal from the striking mines. Prices of food continued to rise. Many people suspected that defeat in the referendum ten months earlier had led advocates of conscription to resort to economic conscription — forcing workers to enlist through a combination of unemployment and high prices. These, some believed, were caused by profiteering and the stockpiling of meat and wheat. And, adding insult to injury, the population was being urged to make unprecedented material sacrifices for the war effort, in an Economy Campaign which culminated in Thrift Week in June 1917. Significantly, the campaign was led by the Victorian Employers' Federation, the conservative People's Party and the equally conservative Australian Women's National League, and was supported by the Chambers of Commerce and Manufactures. Workers, not surprisingly, felt that thrift was a luxury they could ill afford. As one Victorian Legislative Councillor expressed it: 'The Ministry preached thrift to men who were starving.'[16] At the same time, the government increased its repression of free speech and free association, making it more difficult for people to engage in peaceful, lawful forms of civic protest.

Tensions in Melbourne also ran high because of the sectarian bitterness fostered by the presence on the one hand of the Catholic Archbishop Daniel Mannix, and on the other of militant members of the newly formed Victorian Protestant Federation. Religion-based divisions combined with the economic pressures and the legal repression to make many people increasingly willing to resort to desperate measures to improve their position.

All of this might explain why the workers rioted, but it does not explain why women should have taken such a leading role in the process. The women who led the demonstrations were all socialists with long records of militant political activity on issues ranging from female suffrage to anti-conscription. In one sense, then, they were thoroughly 'modern' women, using modern forms of organisation and expression to achieve their well-thought-out aims. In another sense, however, they appealed to a much older aspect of womanhood — that associated with woman's traditional role in the home as housewife and childcarer. Although it is true that large numbers of women, especially in Victoria, had been in the paid workforce since the late nineteenth century, the majority of adult women still played a role which was more concerned with consumption than earning money. That is, as wives of working men, they had to make the money spin out to feed the family and so were more immediately concerned about rising prices than men were — and they were also usually the first to go hungry in hard times. Thus, while women played a *supportive* role in the strikes of the time (these were mostly about men's conditions in the paid workforce), they took a *leading* part in the cost-of-living demonstrations (supported in this case by working men) as this related more specifically to their sphere. Nor were these public outbursts by women something which occurred only in the context of the war. Women, especially mothers, had always led 'bread riots', demanding what they saw as rightfully theirs — affordable food for themselves and their families. The particular economic pressures which caused Melbourne women to protest were a product of the war, but their willingness to demonstrate was not.

Suggestions for study

To discuss

1   Stage a role-play set in a magistrate's court in Sydney at the height of the General Strike of 1917. The following people appear before the magistrate to give their version of events and explain their behaviour:
    -   the wife of a striker, charged with assault
    -   a woman volunteer driver (from a wealthy North Shore family), charged with using abusive language and disturbing the peace
    -   an Irish policeman called in to break up a fight between the above.
    The class may wish to give their 'verdict'.
2   Hold a debate between members of the Women's Peace Army and the Australian Women's National League on the introduction of conscription.

To write about

1   It is 1917 and the Hughes Government has announced a second referendum on the question of conscription. Design two posters, one putting the case for and the other against conscription. Be mindful of who your audience might be and how to make your case most persuasive. You may use visual as well as written text.
2   Choose the persona of a member of the public in 1917. Write a letter to the editor of a daily newspaper expressing your views on the cost-of-living demonstrations in Melbourne. Compare your letters with those written by others in the class.
3   You are an Irish Catholic nun living in a convent in Port Melbourne during the war. You teach in the local parish school and many of your former students have already gone to war. You regularly write home to your family in County Clare, Ireland. Write two such letters: one dated May 1915, the other a year later. Try to capture how your attitudes to the war may have changed between these two dates. (Write freely, in the hope that the censor will not interfere with your letter.)

To research

1   Look through the *Australian Dictionary of Biography* for women involved in the Women's Peace Army, using the names mentioned in this chapter. Do they share any common aspects in their personal backgrounds which may have contributed to their becoming peace activists? Did their work for peace extend beyond the period of the Great War? If so, how?
2   Find out if any of the peace groups or patriotic leagues from the Great War period are still in existence today.

LOSS,
BEREAVEMENT
AND REMEMBRANCE

5

Breaking the news

On 2 December 1915, Major G.F. Stevenson, commanding Officer of the 6th Australian Battery at Gallipoli, wiped the dirt and sweat from his hands and wrote a letter home to Australia. It began in the way so many others did, bearing the most personal of messages to a woman he would never meet. 'It is with extreme regret that I find myself called upon to write to you giving details of the death of your son...'[1]

Brian Lyall had been killed on 29 November. That day the Turkish had bombarded the Australian positions with mortar and artillery fire, causing several casualties and breaking the communication line between the battery observation station and the shore. Major Stevenson had detailed Gunner Lyall to find the break in the telephone wire and mend it. As the young soldier stumbled across the steep and rocky ground, he 'was fully aware of the danger'. There was little cover and the bombardment 'was very heavy' but Lyall, the officer wrote, was a lad determined to do his duty. 'He went on the mission without hesitation or complaint and somewhere in the trenches he was struck by a piece of shell and was buried to his waist in the dirt knocked down by the explosion.' It took several hours for them to find Gunner Lyall, several hours more to carry his broken, bleeding body to the field hospital on the beach. And though Major Stevenson broke the news as gently as he could, it was clear that it took Mrs Lyall's son several hours to die:

I sent my Sergeant Major down to [the beach] the following morning. He was informed that the poor lad had passed away at 2 am. that morning... This news, I assure you, was a great shock to me, as [I thought] his wounds would soon mend and that he would in all probability be sent home. However God's will was otherwise.

We don't know if Mrs. Lyall found much comfort in the thought that God had taken the life of a loving son. We do know, from the worn and crumpled parchment, that she (and her family?) read the Major's letter time and time again. Somehow, knowing how her son died offered some consolation. And the Major was careful to choose words a grieving mother longed to hear. Gunner Lyall was 'the best liked man in the Battery and though one of the youngest he was the manliest of them all...he died as brave and manly as he lived and...the way he did his duty will help to sustain you a little in your grief'. In a way, the Major's letter served to set things to order. It assured a family far away that all that was possible had been done. Lyall's belongings were 'sold by auction to his comrades who bought them up eagerly as

Figure 5.1
Kipling's poem appeared in the Queenslander *surrounded by photographs of the graves of Australian soldiers.*
(*Queenslander*, 22 April 1916)

■ Note the date of publication. Why was the poem printed at that time?

'It is with very much regret...'

In December 1917 Mrs Bromley received the news that her son had died three months earlier. It was some time after that she was notified of his place of burial. These documents are part of a collection devoted to her son's memory.

(Bromley Family Papers, Ms 10145, La Trobe Library, Melbourne)

AUSTRALIAN IMPERIAL FORCE.

IN MEMORY OF

(Name) B R O M L E Y   Roy Phillips.

(No.) 2813. (Rank) L/Sgt

(Unit)   29th Battalion

Interred Hooge Crater Cemetery
Plot 11. Row D. Grave 15

Nearest Railway Station   Ypres.
4 Copies
    Killed at Bapaume
    26.9. 1917.

ROY BROMLEY
29th BTN
KILLED SEPT 1917
BAPAUME

M.308

27.12.17

Dear Mrs Bromley.

It is with very much regret that I now have to inform you that your son has been now reported Killed in Action on the 26th Sept..

I have been hoping against hope that he would turn up alright, but we have just received word from a wounded man who says that both he and your son Roy were together when a shell burst close to them .   This man Private H. A. L. Davies was wounded but your son was killed.

On this information Roy has been reported Killed Please accept my deepest sympathy in your great loss.

There is nothing I can say about Roy that is too good for him, both as a soldier and a man.   He was one of the most dependable men in the Company and one who could always be relied on, no matter what the circumstances were.

When Bapaume fell on the 17th March, I had to go out, well in front of our line to reconnoitre the position.   It was a particularly trying and dangerous task and I selected Roy to come with me.   He worked splendidly there and it was largely due to his courage and initiative that I gained much information for further operations.   Since then he has proved his worth too

Not only was he a fine soldier but he was most popular among the Company.   I am sure I am expressing the feelings of the whole Company, officers, N.C.O's, and men alike when I offer you our deepest sympathy.

Yours on duty

N. G. Gray
Lieut.

■ Do you think Mrs Bromley found comfort in the lieutenant's letter? Why?

■ Why were these documents preserved so long after her own death?

mementos of one they all admired.' And his body was laid out to rest. The boy from Victoria was buried 'in a cemetery close to Ari Burnu on the beach', a chaplain read a service and 'a wooden cross [was] erected on the grave'. For the family, too, there were mementos. Aside from the dead man's letters, watch and diaries, the Major saved 'a silver brandy flask with his name engraved thereon'. It was dated with the week that Lyall enlisted: 'you would value it more than anyone else [possibly] could'. It was not much to remember a lifetime, a lifetime cut tragically short.[2]

It is difficult to know what Brian Lyall's mother thought as she sifted through the memories and belongings, handling the wreckage of a young man's life. The one thing that is certain is that she was not alone in her grief. Of the 330 000 men who served abroad, 60 000 would never return. They were buried close to where they died, in the cemeteries that dot the landscapes of England and Egypt, Gallipoli and France. Over 18 000 bodies were never recovered. Brian Lyall's grave was marked by a simple wooden cross, but for these men there is nothing to spare the anonymity of death. Thousands of names are inscribed on single monuments, and bodies decayed or mutilated beyond recognition were marked with a tombstone reading 'An Australian Soldier: Known to God'. If one assumes that each man had 10 people he was very close to — father, mother, sibling, fiancée, lover, wife, mates — then the war brought bereavement to 600 000 people; about one in every six Australians knew what it was like to experience such loss.

The first news of these men's deaths was a good deal less personal than Major Stevenson's letter. After the landing at Gallipoli or the major battles on the Somme, casualty lists were published in the daily papers. Anxious eyes ran down the alphabet, closing at every name they recognised. But private announcements were even more difficult. 'The message came', one Red Cross worker recalled, 'in a dreaded pink envelope', a few words in thick black telegraphic ink reporting an inestimable loss.[3] Crueller still, she continued was the stiff, quiet voice on the telephone; as mothers put down the heavy receivers it was as if they closed a door on life. But mostly the message was given personally, by a policeman or a parson 'trying to soften the blow'. They never succeeded. Instead, entire communities lived in fear of those slow, deliberate footsteps and a gentle knocking on the door which brought the news of death:

Some women wouldn't open their doors to a clergyman during that first war. I had four boys away, and when I hadn't heard from your father for some months I used to stand at the side of the curtain peeping out the corner of the window so no one would see me watching the road. I was waiting for Mr Nancarrow, our minister; for days I expected him. He did come, and I saw him walk up the hill and look straight at our house. He couldn't see me behind the lace curtain. I must have closed my eyes for the next thing was I saw him go into Mrs Mason's place on the other side of the road. I sat down, plonk! on the settee, I was so drained out. Then I thought, poor Mrs Mason's Harry, that's who it must be, and it was. Mr Nancarrow came and knocked on my door after he told her and asked me to go to her. When the minister did come for me — three times he came — I knew each time which one of the boys it was.[4]

At least Mrs Mason and her neighbour knew the worst. Thousands of mothers were told that their sons were simply 'missing', their bodies swallowed up in the chaos of war. 'Missing' was a kind of limbo; a twilight world between life and death. And 'missing' held terrors even worse than death. One might pray for news that never came, or mourn a life that was quite literally lost. For years most women swung from one extreme to the other; frightened to give up hope but longing to lay a life to rest.

■ Mrs Hope of Melbourne, Victoria, pasted this verse into a scrapbook she kept during the course of the Great War. Why?

Document 5.2

Missing

(Hope Papers, Ms 12598
La Trobe Library, Melbourne)

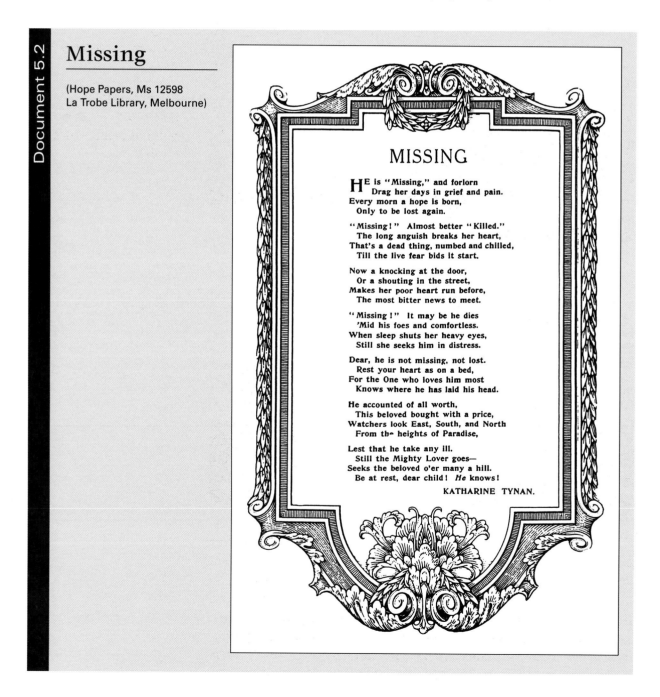

MISSING

HE is "Missing," and forlorn
  Drag her days in grief and pain.
Every morn a hope is born,
  Only to be lost again.

"Missing!" Almost better "Killed."
  The long anguish breaks her heart,
That's a dead thing, numbed and chilled,
  Till the live fear bids it start.

Now a knocking at the door,
  Or a shouting in the street,
Makes her poor heart run before,
  The most bitter news to meet.

"Missing!" It may be he dies
  'Mid his foes and comfortless.
When sleep shuts her heavy eyes,
  Still she seeks him in distress.

Dear, he is not missing, not lost.
  Rest your heart as on a bed,
For the One who loves him most
  Knows where he has laid his head.

He accounted of all worth,
  This beloved bought with a price,
Watchers look East, South, and North
  From the heights of Paradise,

Lest that he take any ill.
  Still the Mighty Lover goes—
Seeks the beloved o'er many a hill.
  Be at rest, dear child! *He* knows!

KATHARINE TYNAN.

Living with grief

It is often assumed that bereavement united women; rich or poor, young or old, wife, sister, mother all shared a common grief. But we should also remember that individual women responded to such loss very differently and that each woman's bereavement could run a whole gamut of emotions. To lose a son or a husband or a brother at war provoked not only sadness but also pride and anger, resignation and denial, confusion and regret.

Figure 5.2

A mother farewells a troop transport (*Queenslander*, 24 October 1914)

■ What is the *Queenslander* saying with this picture? (Note the date.)

How, then, did women respond to death? Throughout the war years, women were discouraged from publicly professing their grief. Mourning had a place, of course, but a soldier's death was not the exclusive concern of his loved ones: soldiers laid down their lives for their country and their king. Grieving mothers were told that this sacrifice was a noble one; it was right and proper men gave their lives for their country and that women 'surrendered up their sons'. In war, the loss of young lives could not be mourned the way they should have been. Grief was substituted with the ideal of 'maternal sacrifice'. The Queensland *National Leader* even argued that the true value of a mother could be measured by the number of boys she sent to death at the Front:

> It is a great pity that all mothers are not of the same mind as Mrs Budgin of Bulimba who has sent three of her sons to the Front. One has been killed in France while the remaining two are still in the trenches. These are her own words: 'If I had twenty sons, I'd send them willingly and if they would not go, I would not own them.'[5]

Women like Mrs Budgin found some comfort in the thought that their children had died for 'Empire'. Indeed, in many cases, a sense of pride almost overwhelmed the sense of loss:

> The mother who gives her son in war is noble, sublime…the noblest thing on earth today… Sometimes I go to the Coo-ee cafe and I chat to women who are suffering a noble martyrdom and my heart thrills with pride at a heroism that seems to me to be stupendously great. They tell me of their boys, of the letters they have had from them and I feel that I am breathing in an atmosphere cleansed by the spirit of a nobility that is sacred.[6]

It might have seemed 'noble' to surrender a son to war; in reality, the suppression of grief could make the loss of loved ones even more difficult to cope with. Memorial notices announced pride in one who had died for his country: 'Such a death was immortality' one boasted, these were 'noble lives, nobly ended'. They were signed, nonetheless by 'sorrowing mothers', or by friends, sisters, aunts 'who miss you so much' and 'who [can] never forget'. Even in the most patriotic of poetry there is often a powerful current of despair and dissatisfaction. In verses like Kathleen Chute-Erson's 'Killed in Action' we hear the voice of women trying to make sense of such untimely death:

Yes, I am proud; I shall not weep, my son —
  Boy of the high brave spirit, who lies slain,
Blent with the earth grown hallowed for the stain
  Of your young life-blood. Boy who on my breast
Has lain, so small, so dear; in infant rest,
  Whose tiny, clinging hands and nestling head
Seemed God and life to me — dear son, now dead.

Son of the strong young frame, the fearless heart,
  Vibrant with life and thought; the coming man,
Shadowed in graver mood; the finished plan
  My mother-love foresaw and knew content.
And when all youthful fire and courage blent,
  You said good-bye, I smiled (Oh, God! that day
Fear clutched my heart!) I would not have you stay.

Boy! you have died as we would have you die.
  Yes, I am proud, my son, I shall not weep;
But, oh! within the hours of broken sleep
  I see your dear loved form, your eyes, your hair,
And clench my arms to clasp and hold you there;
  Then wake, to know the glory you have won,
Yes, I am proud, indeed, but — son, oh, son![7]

Document 5.3

Violet Verses

Violet Day was observed throughout Australia and the British Empire on 22 June each year. It was a day of national remembrance and a chance to raise money for voluntary bodies like the Red Cross. With the end of the war in 1918, Violet Day was effectively replaced with Remembrance Day (11 November) and poppies were substituted for violets. Annie Seager was active in the Cheer-Up Club in Adelaide and a fervent advocate of compulsory military service.

To the dear memory of George Rothwell Seager, whose good-bye was, 'If I stop a bit of German lead, be a sport!'
By His Mother

To-day we wear the clinging violet
In memory of the brave,
While e'er thoughts of fond but proud regret,
Come surging wave on wave.

Some sleep beside the sobbing Dardanelles,
And some in gallant France,
'Mid gardens fair, where medieval bells
Wake echoes of romance.

'Twas fitting that the young and brave should die
To build a nation's name —
That strong, young hands should mould its destiny
In an undying fame.

In morning's Glory or the noon of Life
They fell, our fighting men;
In burning valour — the white heat of strife
They passed beyond our ken.

'Whom the gods love', so the ancients said, 'die young.'
How could it other be?
Would love drag glorious youth through weary years
To age's misery…

Ah! Their's was life — life worthy of a man,
Whose exit was a thrill.
No weary acquiescence in a plan.
That long, dull years must fill…

And we, the mothers, sisters, sweethearts, wives,
Of these, our dear young dead,
Leave with them there the sunshine of our lives,
Lost in the mist of red.

For them no tolling bell, no funeral pall —
(Their's was a common death),
But flowers whose spring-like fragrance touches all,
With love in every breath.

'Far better to have loved and lost', they say,
'Than never loved at all';
For always at some time gold turns to gray,
And evening shadows fall.

We'll strew with thoughts of love and fairest flowers
The path our heroes trod;
We'll bless the precious years that made them ours,
And leave the rest to God.
A. Seager

(Frederick J. Miles, *Cheer Up: A Story of War Work*, Cheer Up Society Incorporated, Adelaide, 1920, pp. 152–4)

Mrs Chute-Erson was divided over the death of her son; others felt an unqualified and bitter loss. The 'noble martyrdom' borne by the women at the Coo-ee Cafe looked very different to the poet Mary Gilmore. A feminist and socialist, she questioned the sense of a war that slaughtered Australia's youth. As the news of the deaths at Gallipoli were announced, she called on the mothers of a nation to give vent to their anguish and their grief:

Dead are the young, the splendid young!
    Creep into bed in the dark and weep;
Broken the bow, the arrow flung
    In the dust where the yard-worms creep.
Call up thy tears
    Where the darkness hears,
Call up thy tears and weep![8]

■ What does Annie Seager's poem tell us about the way pro-Empire women rationalised the loss of loved ones at the Front?

Document 5.4

Roll of Honour

BIRKMYRE. — In loving memory of Sergeant Byron Birkmyre, B Company, 2nd Battalion, 1st A.I.E.F., who was killed in action at Gallipoli, April 27, 1915.

> He fell a hero in the deadly strife,
> For King and country he laid down his life.

Inserted by his sincere comrades, Corp. W. B. Browne and Gunner F. A. Browne.

BRIDGES. — In loving memory of Private James Clyde Bridges, C Company, 3rd Battalion, 1st Australian Imperial Forces, killed in action at the Dardanelles, April 27, 1915. Beloved son of James Bridges and the late Adeline Marie Bridges. Sadly missed. Inserted by his father, sisters and brother, Stella, Daisy, Grace, Bessie, Alma, Adeline, Dorothy, Myrtle, Lillian, and Harold Austin.

COLEMAN. — In loving memory of Pte. W. S. Coleman, who was killed at Gallipoli, April 27, 1915. Inserted by his loving mother and father.

COLEMAN. — In loving memory of Pte. W. S. Coleman, who was killed at Gallipoli, April 27, 1915. Inserted by his loving friends, Mr. and Mrs. Matthews, Ernest and Sydney.

COUTTS. — In loving memory of our dear son, James Alexander (Jim), killed in action at Gallipoli, April 27, 1915, aged 23 years.

COUTTS. — In loving memory of my dear brother, Private Jim Coutts, 4th Battalion, killed in action at Gallipoli, April 27, 1915. Inserted by his loving sister and brother-in-law, Mr. and Mrs. J. R. Wickham, Ryde.

COUTTS. — In sad memory of James (Jimmy) Coutts, who fell amongst the heroes at Anzac, April 27, 1915. Inserted by his sorrowing friend, Gerty Seaton.

COUTTS. — A sincere tribute to the memory of Private J. A. Coutts, killed in action at Gallipoli, April 27, 1915. He gave his young life for King and country. Inserted by Mr. and Mrs. Parkinson and family, Tempe.

COUTTS. — In loving memory of Private James A. Coutts, killed in action at the Dardanelles, April 27, 1915. Inserted by his sincere friends, Mr. and Mrs. W. Morris.

GAMBLE. — A tribute to the memory of my best friend, Archie Gamble, killed at the Dardanelles on or about April 27, 1915. Inserted by his old mate, Arthur Kerslake.

KEMP-HARCOURT. — In loving memory of Beric Vercelles Kemp-Harcourt (Sous-Lieut. Vercelles), who fell at Ypres between April 25 and May 3, 1915. Inserted by his relatives and friends.

McFEELY. — A tribute of love to the memory of Sergeant-Major George Edward McFeely, who was killed at Ypres, in France, on April 27, 1915. Inserted by his friend, Herb. Parsons, Wollongong.

McLELLAN. — In loving memory of my dear son Donald, aged 29, who gave his life for the Empire, at Gallipoli, April 27, 1915.

> You answered the call of your country,
>   But the voice of the cable tells
> That a dauntless lad in a khaki suit
>   Was killed at the Dardanelles.
> We mourn your loss, but your actions
>   Sweet balm to your loved ones bring,
> For he's ever a hero the man who dies
>   For his country, God, and King.

Inserted by his loving mother.

McLELLAN. — In loving memory of our dear brother, Donald (Don), who was killed in action at the Dardanelles, April 27, 1915.

> If we had known when last we lightly parted
> That during life our hands would clasp no
>   more,
> That each who said farewell so cheerful-
>   hearted
> Would find the grief the future held in store,
> How different would have been our solemn
>   parting
> From that which only saw a brief adieu,
> How would the tears of mutual sorrow starting
> Have dimmed each fleeting moment that we
>   knew.

Inserted by his loving brother, Charlie, and sister-in-law, Queenie, and nephews, Mal, Jim, Allen, Ray, Reg.

McLELLAN. — In loving memory of Corporal D. M. McLellan, killed at Dardanelles, April 27, 1915, 13th Battalion. Inserted by his loving brother and sister-in-law, William and Minnie McLellan.

MULLIGAN. — In loving memory of my dear brother, Leo Terrance Mulligan, who died of wounds received in action at Gallipoli, April 27, 1915, aged 23 years.

> He fell a hero in the deadly strife,
> For King and country he laid down his life.

Inserted by his only sister, Katie Mulligan. R.I.P.

MULLIGAN. — In loving memory of my dear friend, Leo Terrance Mulligan, who died of wounds received in action at Gallipoli, April 27, 1915, aged 23 years. R.I.P. Inserted by his sincere friend, Louie.

ROBERTSON. — In loving memory of Private William Robertson, killed in action in the Dardanelles, on April 27, 1915. Inserted by his sorrowing wife.

SHEPHERD. — In loving memory of my dear son, J. L. Shepherd, 4th Batt., 1st A.I.F., killed in action, Dardanelles, April 27, 1915. Inserted by his loving father.

SHEPHERD. — In loving memory of L.-C. John L. Shepherd, H.Q. Signaller, 4th Batt., 1st Infantry Brigade, killed in action at Dardanelles, April 27, 1915. Inserted by brother and sister-in-law, Robert and Ada.

SHEPHERD. — In memory of my sincere friend, L.-C. John L. Shepherd, H.Q. Signaller, 4th Batt., 1st Infantry Brigade, killed in action at the Dardanelles, April 27, 1915. Inserted by his friend J. W. Monk.

(*Sydney Morning Herald* 27 April 1916)

Supporters of the war effort sought to ennoble the deaths; soldiers 'fell' nobly in battle, they 'rested' in some corner of a foreign field, their 'duty nobly done'. A close friend of those who experienced the horrors of war, Gilmore wrote 'The Mother' on the anniversary of the Gallipoli landing in 1917. There was no dignity in 'a hero's death' at all:

■ What do these messages tell us about Australian families' responses to death?

> Out in the dust
>   He lies;
> Blood in his mouth,
>   Dust in his eyes.
>
> I stood at the door
>   Where he went out,
> Full-grown man,
>   Ruddy and stout.
>
> I heard the march
>   Of the tramping feet,
> Slow and steady
>   Come down the street.
>
> The beat of the drum
>   Was clods on the heart
> For all that the regiment
>   Looked so smart.
>
> I heard the crackle
>   Of hasty cheers,
> As they rose like the breaking
>   Of unshed tears.
>
> And just for a second
>   As he went by,
> I had sight of his face
>   And the flash of his eye.
>
> He died a hero's death,
>   They said,
> When they came to tell me
>   My boy was dead.
>
> But out in the street
>   A dead dog lies,
> Blood in his mouth
>   Dust in his eyes.[9]

It is difficult to recreate the private world of grief and mourning but, again, the memorial columns of the daily papers may well tell us more about Australian women's response to death than the heroic stoicism fostered by the conservative press. Often they give grisly details; men die in battle, or of wounds or are poisoned by gas. A hero's grave looked fine to the patriotic poets; but many a mother was troubled by the thought of bodies draped only in the clothes they died in, of 'the cold clay' closing 'on the beautiful head'. There was a fear that men died without comfort, without a chance to make their peace with those they loved. Private Fredrick Allen Dodson was wounded in the landing on Gallipoli and died at just 19 years of age. Although over a thousand men died with him, 'a loving sister' knew he met his God alone:

No one he loved was by his side
    To hear his last faint sigh
Or whisper just one loving word,
    Before he closed his eyes
He bade no one his last good-bye,
    He waved his hand to no-one,
His spirit fled before we knew
    That from us he had gone.[10]

Figure 5.3

Postcards with messages like this were popular during the Great War.
(Ferguson Papers, Ms 3637, National Library of Australia)

■ What does it tell us about the feelings of those left at home?

Often there was not one tribute but many. The 'In Memorial' notices to Pte W.E. (Darby) Veitch who died of wounds at Villers-Bretonneux took up half a column of the *Sydney Morning Herald*. Darby was sorely missed by father, brothers, uncles, and mates but the most loving words were those placed by women. His mother remembered the touch of a child she raised to manhood:

Could I, his mother, have clasped his hand
    The son I loved so well
Or kissed his brow when death was near,
    And whispered, My son, Farewell.
I seem to see his dear, sweet face
    Through a mist of anxious tears
But a mother's part is a broken heart
    And a burden of lonely years.

His sister Amy and his young niece Rita clung to his letters and photographs, all that was left of his life:

Only a few lines from the trenches,
    With the hand of the writer grown cold;
But his memory is written in letters of love
    In the hearts of those at home.

Another sister, Mary, imagined the grave she might 'never see' — 'may some kind hand/ in that far off land/ strew some flowers there for me'. And Ethel said goodbye as best she could:

Farewell to our dear brother
    Sweet thoughts of you we'll keep
Although one year has passed away
    Our grief is just as deep.[11]

Ethel was as good as her word. Memorial notices to young Darby continued to appear year after year. (Well after the Second World War, sisters and daughters cherished the memories of dead men from the First; then the columns grew large again with a new generation of dead.)

Burying the dead

Mary and Ethel never visited their brother's grave. Australia's soldiers were buried in foreign soil, in places few had ever heard of, thousands of miles from home. Their graves were managed by the Australian Government; even before the war was over the War Graves Commission began the solemn task of commemorating the dead. Massive cemeteries were established on the site of former battlefields: Fromelles, Pozières, Villers-Bretonneux. On a once-scarred and blackened landscape rose thousands and thousands of simple white tombstones, row after row of soldiers' graves. As monuments to the dead they are awesome and impressive. The King himself unveiled the towering memorial at Villers-Bretonneux: flanked by dignitaries and ministers, he stood, he said, 'on hallowed ground'.[12] It is ground that belongs neither to kings nor governments but to those whose loved ones lie there.

Unlike those other nations, Australian families were invited to choose inscriptions for the graves. There is no more moving testimony to the terrible loss of war than the words chiselled into the stark white stones. Deaths are described as noble and the dead men as heroes; men gave their lives 'for Australia', 'for England', 'for Freedom' and most of all 'for others' — they fought 'to save us all'. In many inscriptions one senses the pride of those they left behind them. Sgt F.L. Partridge of the 59th Battalion died on 26 April 1918, 26 years of age — 'A Soldier and a Man, One of Australia's Best'. Private A.J. McCaffrey won the Military Medal for bravery in battle — 'A brave soldier, a loving son, a mother's sacrifice, for duty done'. G.S. French was barely 18 when he died, just a few months before the end of the war, but his mother and father found solace in his sacrifice — 'He died as few men have a chance to die/ fighting for God and Liberty.'

While pride in such men is evident enough, an equally common theme is anger at their loss. Indeed the great distance from home made these final messages to loved ones all the more anguished. Many deny death: wives will not say goodbye, mothers refuse to part from sons. Buried in the spring of 1918, Sgt Miles was not dead; rather, he is 'still living, still loving, still ours'. Private Scott 'is not dead/ for such as my noble husband/ lives forever'. These men 'death cannot sever' from loved ones. 'Love remembered lasts forever'. Many inscriptions record the loss of 'our only darling son', and some, it seems, record their final words: 'Tell mother I'll be there', Private Battagline's gravestone reads, 'in answer to her prayer'. And for all the talk of honour, all the pride in King and Country, there is also disillusion and fear. Among the acres of dead, Private W.L. Rae's headstone speaks of futility and incomprehension: 'Another life lost/ Hearts broken for what?'

Hearts broken in war never mended. Kenneth Grant Duke died in January 1919, almost a lifetime ago. His grave is to be found in a little churchyard in England, not far from the site of a military hospital where Australian nurses served. The inscription reads 'Always Remembered'. In September 1994, 75 years after his death, a bouquet of fresh flowers was placed on his grave. The message read:

A very dear and cheerful brother
who died so young and so far away
Remembered lovingly by your sisters
 Joyce and Thora
 of Melbourne Australia.

Today, the graves of Australian soldiers do not seem quite so far away. In an age of jet planes, many families make uncertain 'pilgrimages', visiting the final resting place of uncles, grandparents, or fathers they probably never knew. Many place poppies on the graves of unknown soldiers, hoping perhaps that the bodies buried beneath them are somehow 'theirs'. And most leave a message in the cemetery register. Again, the task of expressing grief falls (usually) to the women. 'In memory of the Arnotts', Joy Jansen travelled from Canberra to Amiens; her hand shook as she scribbled on the page. Sarah Crowley thanked the French caretaker who weeded the graves around her; somewhere among those rows and rows of dead her great-grandfather lay. Kate Richardson of the Monash University regiment felt proud to be a soldier: 'Lest We Forget' seemed an appropriate tribute, but the letters are all jumbled from the emotion of the visit. Karen Ingu, on the other hand, relived the grief of mothers, sisters, sweethearts: 'An immense loss to Australian families', she wrote, 'Vive la Republic!' Perhaps she had seen that bitter protest on Private Rae's grave.

Document 5.5

To the Unknown Hero

The Unknown Soldier acquired a kind of hero status as the war progressed. In 1920, he was paid the highest tribute of all when the remains of an unidentified British soldier were interred at the entrance of Westminster Abbey.

We hold no record, boy, of your brave deed;
We know not how 'twas done, nor in what need
Your courage leapt to life!
We only know you won a name,
And that you bravely played the game,
And conquered in the strife!

We try to picture, boy, just how 'twas done:
We hear the shriek of shell, the boom of gun,
And shudder in our dream!
Was it at night you braved the foe,
Or while the evening's sunset glow.

We do you honour, boy, howe'er it was,
Our hearts are full for you, more so because

We know not who you are!
We know you are some mother's son,
And a splendid Cross you've won
Which glistens like a star!

And though your record, boy, is not on earth,
And though no book of fame sets forth your
    worth,
Your heart need not be sad!
A surer book is kept on high,
And your brave deed will never die —
Rejoice, then, and be glad!

You are a hero, boy, though yet unknown:
I would Australia's arms were round you thrown
In proud and loving care!
We cannot do too much for you,
A nation's homage is your due,
A nation's grateful prayers!
Caroline Louisa Daniel
Mordialloc
(Hope Papers, Ms 12598, La Trobe Library, Melbourne)

■ Why does Caroline Daniel, a woman from Melbourne, glorify a man she has never met?
■ In what ways does Caroline Daniel's view of the battlefield differ from M.E.F's (Document 5.6)? How do you explain the different perspectives of the two women?

Document 5.6

The Mother's Soul

I was a woman of the human race,
Who owned the whole world for her native place:
And by my woman love I gave him birth,
My happy boy, to live his term on earth;
They took him from his honest toil and me,
And called another's son his enemy.

I was a woman, and my heart well knew
'Twas lies that sent him forth the crime to do;
'Twas lies that laid him staring to the skies,
His bayonet red, the film upon his eyes;
They took him from his happy life and me,
And made another's son his enemy.

I was the mother of that other's son,
She my son's mother, having mothered one;
And there they lay, whom we had given life,
Stark, with steel red from fratricidal strife:
They took her son from her…took mine from me,
And called each son the other's enemy.

Forth sped their life; with theirs our quivering
    souls
(When brothers kill, death takes quadruple toll),
Ay, more! All human motherhood makes mourn
For generations of their noble sons unborn,
The children that shall never open eyes
Because they made our children enemies.
M.E.F.
(*Woman Voter*, 10 February 1916)

Figure 5.4

An early sculpture of the Man and the Donkey (*Queenslander,* 10 May 1919)

■ The historian Peter Cochrane has argued that Simpson's simple but heroic story had a special appeal to women and children. Would you agree? Why or why not?

Honouring the dead

Honouring the dead was not confined to the cemeteries where they lay. Even before the war had ended, families and townships, clubs, schools and businesses set about commemorating those who had made the 'Supreme Sacrifice'.

Honour rolls in workshops, schools and offices — initially established to stimulate recruitment — soon had neat crosses carved beside the names of many who had gone away but would not return. Monumental masons were quick to seize on a promising new market as families erected memorials in local cemeteries. Crosses and angels would not do for these fallen warriors: the empty tombs are marked with swords, rifles, bugles or the phrase that grew to be a legend: 'Killed in the Dardanelles'. The first public monuments were also sited in cemeteries. When Victor Denton died — 'A Queensland Hero' — in the Dardanelles, the residents of Nobby erected a marble column to his memory.[13] The pillar is 'broken' near the base, signifying a life cut short.

Soon, memorials like this one were placed squarely in the public domain. Even before the war had ended, many townships had their own little monument triumphantly planted beside the post office or town hall. With peace, the production of war memorials became something of an industry. Councils and citizens chose their particular tribute from catalogues of statues, pillars, crosses and plaques. Many of the stone diggers 'standing to rest' in towns and suburbs were ordered *en masse* from workshops in Italy — 'an invading army', a disgruntled American artist noted, destined to occupy all the Allies' shores.[14]

Looking at them today, one might think that these memorials had little to do with women. The stiff white soldier, the cross and the sword, the upright pillar and the captured enemy guns; all these are very masculine symbols, commemorating battles only men had fought. Very few memorials mention the women that served in the Great War; the names 'that live forever more' are almost invariably the names of men. But that is a very simplistic reading. Women were at the centre of all these commemorations. It was women who raised the money to build the monuments; who rallied together their communities to lobby local government; who made the wreathes for the ceremonies; and who gathered each year to remember sons, lovers and fathers they had lost. Often it was a widow or the mother of a soldier killed abroad who was chosen to unveil the monument; the memorial was to symbolise not just the 'supreme sacrifice' of 'the fallen' but also the sacrifice women had made of those to whom they had given life. And the monument was a surrogate grave as well. When mothers and wives laid wreathes beneath the grim tally of engraved names, their thoughts were often far away, with bodies blending with the soil of Gallipoli and Egypt, England and France.

Document 5.7

For Valour

Not in the field alone are honours won,
Nor where the bullet stays the robbing breath,
Where screaming shells rain 'neath a blackened
   sun,
And all is smoke — and destiny — and death.

Not in the trench alone the crown, the cross,
For those who eager took the challenge up:
Pangs, worse than death, are theirs who face the
   loss,
Who stay behind — to drink the bitter cup.

In homes bereft, far in the country's hush
Round once glad hearths, amid the cities pent,
In lonely homes, grief stricken, in the bush;
'Tis there I'd have the Cross for Valour sent.

For women are not bred to lust of war,
To slaughter and to hate — and yet they give
With open hands, their very life and more,
That Right and Truth and Justice still may live.

The men they bore — the hardy, valiant ones,
At duty's call, prayer-clasped, their frail hands
   sped,

Who once upon their breasts were 'little sons',
Who now lie numbered with the glorious dead.

High on the altar of their country's pride
Brave hearts who placed their all now patient wait
To prove the end, for which their sons have died:
The strength of Right and Truth, inviolate.

With steady eyes, they face the darkened years
When war shall cease, and peace be ours again.
What of the mother grief, too deep for tears?
What of their empty arms outstretched in vain?

Mothers of men — to whom no dawn of peace
Shall bring the sons, who once against their breast
Were held, soft clasped, for whom shall never
   cease
The aching longing and wild unrest.

Far from the reeking cannon's hymn of hate,
In quiet homes, the bitter issue won.
Give them the Cross for Valour, those who wait.
Fronting the wreck of all that was their own.
Carew Smyth
Brisbane

(Hope Papers, Ms 12598, La Trobe Library,
Melbourne)

Often the names on a monument tell their own tale of a family's sacrifice. The Redfern Memorial in Sydney records over thirty of 'the fallen'. There are two Kellys listed, two Hoods, two Clements, two Gerahtys, two Hydes. Anne Hunter lost all three sons in the space of as many years: two were buried in the gullies of Gallipoli; the youngest, William, was killed in action in France. The O'Brien and Sale families also lost three sons. An entire generation was blighted.

The suffering of war is by no means confined to the soldiers who fought; women's suffering (as the poem 'For Valour' suggests) continued long after battles had been won or lost. It is not surprising that women figure so prominently in popular memories of Anzac Days. Growing up in Melbourne, caught in the generation that had 'just escaped the war', Graham McInnes remembered them quite clearly: 'Bereaved mothers, as stern-faced as Volumnia, attended service standing erect and dry-eyed, their bosoms stitched with their dead sons' medals.' Grim and silent, they towered over the bodies of 'maimed and crippled [veterans who] sat on chairs or hobbled on crutches'. It was a pity, McInnes concluded, that Anzac Day was often portrayed as a chance for returned soldiers to indulge in a bit of 'a booze up'. In fact, it was almost a 'religious' experience, where men remembered mates and women grieved the loss of loved ones.[15]

■ What does this poem tells us about the writer's view of the different natures and roles of men and women?
■ Do you think the poem would have helped women to be reconciled to their loss? Explain your response.

Anzac Day

This and Document 5.9 are newspaper reports of the first Anzac Day commemoration in Brisbane. Read both accounts and then answer the questions.

Impressive commemoration in Brisbane

A sob seemed to shake the community yesterday as it stepped forward and placed a simple flower on the graves of the gallant men slain on the heights of Gallipoli. The little cemetery and the trenches where they lie buried are silent and deserted now, but loving thoughts clustered round that spot, sacred to the memory of the brave, and many a silent prayer went up on behalf of dear ones left mourning, while the heartfelt hope was breathed that in this hour of fiery trial the nation might be worthy of its fallen heroes, who had blazed a bright and shining way at Anzac. The dominant note was one of mourning — it could not have been otherwise — but mingled with it, and breaking through like the sunlight glinting through the rain clouds which gathered and yielded soft showers during the day, was the feeling of triumph and pride that Australia has such worthy sons. The observance of Anzac Day was largely of a religious nature, for where the realities of life and death are concerned they find fittest expression in the ordinances of the churches, and the early part of the day was given up to divine service in the camps, followed by similar affecting services in the principal city churches, where soldiers and civilians, standing together, mourned the dead and paid a tribute of silent respect. During the afternoon there was an imposing march of troops through the city, witnessed by immense crowds — probably the largest that have ever assembled in the metropolis — and…impressive public meetings in the Exhibition Building and other halls. The day was observed as a bank holiday, in which the banks, insurance offices, and public-service participated, and the shops which were open closed in the afternoon sufficiently long to allow employees to witness the military procession, whilst most of the wholesale firms shut at midday.

Spectacular march of troops

The march of the troops was the biggest and most impressive yet witnessed in Brisbane, no fewer than 6434 soldiers taking part… Toward half-past 2 o'clock the crowd became so dense at this point [in front of the GPO] that the police, of whom there was a strong force, and a number of military who were assisting them, became utterly powerless to deal with the pushing and struggling mass of humanity which surged to and fro, completely blocking the roadway. A space was cleared through the crowd by mounted troopers on the arrival of his Excellency the Governor, but, despite all effort, the crowd closed in behind the carriage, and again filled the roadway. Several women were crushed, and fainted, and the services of the Ambulance were requisitioned. The arrival of the returned soldiers, some of whom subsequently formed a guard of honour, was the signal for an outburst of cheering. The men, many of whom belonged to famous fighting regiments, the crossed swords on their shoulders denoting special distinction, had great difficulty in passing through the crowd which was mainly comprised of women…

(*Queenslander*, 26 April 1916)

■ Why did such large numbers of people view the procession and why was the crowd 'mainly comprised of women'?

■ Why did Archbishop Duhig believe women as well as men deserved medals?

■ Was Anzac Day just a day of mourning; or did the commemoration serve some other purpose?

Not all the memorials raised to Australia's dead were edifices of rock and stone. Libraries, town halls, recreation reserves and even swimming pools were built to honour fallen soldiers. All of these amenities served useful purposes. They were also a way of incorporating women and children into what we might call 'the politics of remembrance'. War memorials, women often argued, were not just for the dead; they should serve the living as well. After all, it was for the living that 'their boys' had died.

The Avenues of Honour which line the approach to towns and suburbs throughout Australia are another illustration of how women shaped the commemoration of war. Marked by plaques bearing the names of dead soldiers, the tall poplars and flowering gums were individual as well as collective memorials. Like the statues, they provided surrogate graves for men whose bodies lay

Document 5.9

Gathering in the exhibition hall: Magnificent tribute to our soldiers

Admiration of their heroism and endurance: 'The dead shall not have fought in vain.'

The day's proceedings in Brisbane were closed with a magnificent gathering in the Exhibition Hall. The heroic deeds on Gallipoli and all they stood for were graphically pictured in words, and if the meeting was less solemn than the memorial services in the morning, there was one particularly moving period, when at 9 o'clock, the vast assemblage stood for a minute in silent prayer for the dead, and when the organ tones broke in with 'Dead March' there were many wet eyes.

Big in numbers and representative in character, the meeting recognised the sacrifices and devotion to duty of the men of Anzac, breathed sympathy with the bereaved, and made a stirring appeal to others to follow the example of those who had assisted to retain the blessings of liberty…

His Grace Archbishop Duhig moved, — 'This meeting voices heartfelt sympathy with those whose loved ones laid down their lives for the Empire, and assures the bereaved, and the soldiers who have suffered, of the undying grati-tude of the people who through that sacrifice retain the blessings of liberty, enhanced by a fuller sense of nationhood and closer and stronger union with the other portions of the British Dominions.' The resolution, he said, was one which must find a responsive chord in the heart of every person present, and throughout Queensland. It expressed sympathy with those whose husbands and sons and brothers had fallen in battle. It expressed undying gratitude to those who had suffered and laid down their lives for a noble cause, and it affirmed that through their sacrifice we had come to a higher and greater sense of nationhood. It was difficult to know which was to be most admired, the courage and endurance of men who performed those deeds of superlative glory or the sacrifice of the mothers who gave their sons freely to the service of the war and on behalf of a noble cause. We went along in our peaceful lives, and we thought our Australian mothers were overindulgent, and that their children were being spoilt. But he was proud to say that the mothers and sisters and wives of Australia could be placed side by side with the very best womanhood in the Empire. (Loud applause.) They had done their duty nobly and well, and he would like to advocate that the mothers who had given sons to the Empire should be decorated in a special manner. (Applause.)

(*Courier* [Brisbane], 26 April 1916)

so far away. These totems of death and sacrifice were also powerful symbols of life and renewal. It is not surprising they were located at the entry to many townships; the young growth symbolised the boys marching home. Many of these trees were planted and tended by women. The planting of trees served an important purpose for women unable to bury their dead: just as poppies grew on the blood-soaked battlefields, these trees were nourished with wives' and mothers' tears.

Women's influence over the way the dead were remembered was sometimes controversial. The style chosen for Sydney's Anzac memorial, for instance, reveals a number of competing interests. The way women wanted to express their mourning differed from the style of commemoration favoured by church, government and many surviving soldiers as well.

A memorial had been mooted from as early as 1916 and a building fund was established towards the end of the war. By the early 1920s several thousand pounds had been donated but few people could agree on where the memorial should be situated or what precise form it would take.

Figure 5.5
Dora Ohlfsen's bas relief on the war memorial in Mornington, Victoria
(Photograph courtesy E.W. Scates)

■ What do you think the woman in the sculpture is meant to represent?

The state government favoured some form of edifice at the southerly approach to the Harbour Bridge; the style would be grand, triumphant and certain to match any shrine they might build down in Melbourne. Many grieving parents hoped a memorial would be built near the wharves at Woolloomooloo — it was there that they had said goodbye to children they would never see again. The form of the memorial raised just as many problems. By the early 1920s, the Returned Sailors and Soldiers Imperial League (forerunner of the RSL) was already a powerful political lobby. It favoured a club house for its members, equipped with special facilities for those maimed by war. Mothers who had lost their sons saw the matter rather differently. Dr Mary Booth and her League of Anzac Women wanted a place where they could go to pray and remember — not another city bar frequented exclusively by men. Women, Dr Booth argued, had just as much say in the matter as those who had fought the war. Not only had they given their sons, they had also raised most of the money. It was given 'for a memorial to the fallen...for something national and permanent and of great architectural beauty'.[16] It was not until 1929 that the arguments were settled — the memorial would be a Shrine of Remembrance and located in one of the few remaining open spaces of the city, Hyde Park.

The conception and building of the memorial presented yet another set of problems and again the divisions fell along broad

Document 5.10

Anzac Day at Sydney Girls High School

On Anzac Day we again had the privilege of listening to a most inspiring address by Rev. P.A. Micklem, M.A., D.D. Dr. Micklem, who has recently returned from England, spoke of his visit to the tomb of the Unknown Warrior in Westminster Abbey. 'The Great War', he said, 'was the common soldier's war, and it brought out the splendid character, the capacity for endurance, and the bravery and heroism of the rank and file, who are representative of that great host who gave their lives in the war for king and country.'

'Anzac Day', he went on to say, 'which commemorates the day when Australian troops first went into action in Australia's greatest war-day — a splendid feat of arms which serves not only to corroborate the verdict of time, that such a deed as was wrought upon that day would be memorable in the history of any nation, but also signifies the birth of the Australian nation, and is therefore a day to be associated with thoughts of love, gratitude and reverence. It is a day, also, to be placed high in the annals of the history of this land, for it was then that Australia came to a new realisation that she was no longer a mere part of a large political fabric, but now occupied an honoured position among the nations of the world — a recognition which took technical form at the assembly of the League of Nations, where she takes her full responsible place in the discussions of the world at Geneva every year.'

'Our kith and kin', said Dr. Micklem, 'who laid down their lives appeal to us to carry on that noble tradition of service and self-sacrifice by a willingness to give ourselves to the cause for which they died — to secure the freedom and privileges we enjoy today; and we must realise that, even more than her manhood, it is the girl-hood and womanhood of a nation which are to shape its destiny, and the character of its fathers and brothers. One of the greatest and best men there has ever been, Abraham Lincoln, said of his mother:— "All that I am or ever hope to be, I owe to my angel mother."'

Dr. Micklem reminded us that 'it is for every girl and woman of today, therefore, to leave such a tradition behind her — with those men-children whose lives are in her keeping. Where shall we learn such lessons but at school, which in its turn prepares us for the greater school of life?'

The concluding thought of the address was that the history of Australia is not the record of a mere hundred and forty years — it is the history of the thousand years of the British nation, of the greatness and grandeur of her past, which is also the greatness and grandeur of our past. And we must note not only the recent, but also the 'dark backward and abysm of time', carrying the imagination further back than the first Anzac Day to the beginning of imperial history, that we may learn and make the knowledge of benefit to Australia.

Norah E. Mathews (4C)

(*High School Chronicle*, Sydney Girls High School, October 1925)

gender lines. According to the architect, Bruce Dellit, the memorial was predominantly a tribute to men: 'It must be strong, original and essentially masculine, for while women took part in the war...the conflict was mainly the concern of men.'[17] But women's contributions could not be so easily marginalised. The most powerful of the friezes depicts nurses ministering to the fallen; they are symbols of life and tenderness in a battleground filled with suffering and death. Three of the four massive buttresses which support the building incorporate statues of lieutenants from the Air Force, Navy and Army, symbolising the services, all depicted in battle dress. The fourth buttress features the figure of a matron in her hospital cape; again, 'feminine' symbols of caring and mercy balance the 'male' portents of war and death.[18] And images of women dominate the Hall of Silence located in the very heart of the memorial.

■ How did Dr Micklem make Anzac Day relevant 'for every girl and every woman'?
■ What part were women expected to play in perpetuating the legend of Anzac?

All of these sculptures were executed by Rayner Hoff, an English-born artist who had seen 'too much of war to glorify it'. Originally, the Hall of Silence was to feature the body of a man lying prone across a bird of prey; Hoff offered an entirely new conception. Three female figures (mother, sister and wife) carry the naked body of a slaughtered soldier; he is their 'best beloved'; their grim, mourning faces are steeled against their loss. One holds a baby as well as the shield supporting the soldier; women — the givers of life — are juxtaposed again against war and the coming of death. It captures, Hoff explained, the 'spirit' of women's sacrifice:

Figure 5.6

Plaster cast of 'The Crucifixion of Civilisation', originally intended for the Sydney War Memorial
(*Sun*, 25 May 1932)

■ Why did church leaders find Rayner Hoff's sculpture so offensive? Do you agree with their judgement?

Thousands of women, although not directly engaged in war activities, lost all that was dearest to them — sons they had borne and reared, husbands, fathers of their children, friends, and lovers. There was no acknowledgment of them in casualty lists of wounded, maimed and killed. They endured all men's sacrifice quietly. In this spirit I have shown them, carrying their load, the sacrifice of their menfolk.[19]

To shift the focus of a national war memorial away from the suffering of men and towards that of women was controversial enough. Even more alarming was Hoff's proposal for another group sculpture beneath the great windows of the exterior. 'The Crucifixion of Civilisation' depicted the massive figure of a naked woman, stretched across a cross formed by a sword. Wounded and dead soldiers are heaped at her feet.

The Calvary of 1914 [Hoff wrote] is the development of [an idea] I had [in the trenches] in France. The group symbolises the destruction of Civilisation by Mars, the immemorial God of War. Adolescent Peace is depicted crucified on the armaments of the ravisher and destroyer. The symbolism is simple and clear — the cross form supporting the armour of war, the Greek helmet animalistically gaping over the sagging head of Peace, the cuirass (body armour) hard and brutal in contrast with the lithe woman's body. Helplessly bound, she droops above the soldier dead.[20]

The exhibition of this work prompted noisy protest from church leaders throughout the state. Nude men had long symbolised the sacrifice of war; but a nude woman was another matter entirely. The theme of crucifixion was seen as particularly offensive. Christians, Archbishop Sheehan explained, looked to the cross as a 'symbol of redemption', not as a portrayal of the horror of war. And then there was the reference 'to the rape and destruction of civilisation' — surely that was not what the Empire's victory was about. 'The Crucifixion of Civilisation' was never completed and now even the temporary plaster cast has been lost. Its suppression seemed to devalue women's suffering. One 'Mother of Three' thought it telling that the Archbishop protested over the nakedness of the woman when surely the real obscenity was the heaped dead men at her feet.[21]

Suggestions for study

To discuss

1   In the 1920s, Australian families were asked to compose the inscriptions for the graves of loved ones buried overseas. Your family has lost three members, including an only daughter and the youngest son. Mother, father and the remaining sons must decide what the inscriptions will say. Form family groups to discuss possible wordings. NOTE: Not all members of the family supported the war and one of the sons is a returned soldier.

2   It is 1919 and a committee has been formed to raise a war memorial in your home town. Among its members are returned soldiers, women who have lost loved ones, church figures and politicians. What form will the memorial take? The choices include a captured enemy gun, a stone soldier, and a community hall. Debate the virtues of these (and other) options and come to a decision.

To write about

1   You are one of the diggers ordered to attack the Turkish trenches at Lone Pine, Gallipoli. You know your chances of survival are slim. A few hours before the battle commences you exchange a last letter home with one of your mates, to be posted in the event of your death. What does it say?

2   You are the mother of an Australian soldier killed at Lone Pine. As next of kin, you are the first to hear of your son's death. Your daughter lives in another state. Write a letter to her, breaking the news of her brother's death.

3   You are one of the nurses serving in India during the war. One of your colleagues has died and, because of an official oversight, there is no commemorative plaque on her grave. You decide to write to the Australian Government asking for some memorial for your friend. What does your letter say?

4   You were engaged to an Australian soldier (or nurse) killed in France in 1916. Write a poem to his/her memory.

To research

1   Almost 80 years after the end of the war, the Australian Government decided to bring home the body of an unknown Australian soldier from France for burial at the Australian War Memorial. Find out why this decision was made. Do you think it was a good idea?

2   Organise a school excursion, if possible, to the Australian War Memorial in Canberra. Inspect the displays and visit the grave of the unknown soldier. Afterwards, interview class members and your teachers to find out their reactions. Which sections of the Memorial did they find most moving? Why?

3   Survey your family and friends. Did any of them lose relatives on either side in the Great War? Do they have any surviving letters, photographs or memorabilia? How do they preserve these important historical sources?

4   Find out what you can about your local (or the nearest) war memorial. When was it built? Who raised the money to build it? Who designed it? Who officiated at the opening ceremony? The local Returned Services League, local library or historical society might be able to help.

THE ENEMY AT HOME

6

Venereal disease

At the height of the European conflict an article was published by a Sydney academic entitled 'The Enemy in Our Midst: Venereal Diseases'.[1] The problem of VD was no isolated fancy of a man removed from the mainstream of the war effort, but a real concern to legislators and social reformers. Military authorities knew from past experience that soldiers, sex and syphilis often went together, with disastrous consequences for the efficiency of the troops. The 'Anzac heroes' were no exception. Their first experience of combat was not on the beaches of Gallipoli but in the brothels of Cairo, where they engaged in public brawls, burning and looting. The first war casualties to be sent home were not suffering from enemy gunfire but from what were often referred to as 'self-inflicted' wounds — that is, venereal diseases contracted through illicit sex.

In the past, military authorities had recognised what they saw as a 'natural tendency' on the part of troops to seek sexual release and had attempted to provide them with access to 'safe' prostitutes. In the nineteenth century, special legislation was passed (known as Contagious Diseases Acts) in Britain and many of its colonies (including Queensland, Tasmania and Victoria) to force prostitutes to undergo regular medical inspection and treatment. It is not surprising, then, to find prostitutes again targeted when it became apparent that there were many cases of VD among the members of the First AIF.

Even before the troops had left Australia, it was found that some of them were infected. In Western Australia in 1915, infected recruits blamed Perth's brothels for their condition. Although that state did not have contagious diseases legislation, the authorities acted quickly to contain 'the menace'. The military officials contacted the Government Medical Officer who worked quietly with local police to force known prostitutes to move into brothels in Roe Street (near the police station) where they could be closely supervised and given regular medical examinations. Even when this illegal practice became publicly known, the police, with the help of certain magistrates, continued to imprison any prostitutes found to be suffering from disease.

The anxiety about the spread of VD became more acute once the troops reached Egypt, where they contracted different strains of the disease. A Western Australian Government minister, Mr R.H. Underwood, felt that drastic measures were called for 'to combat this scourge', otherwise 'Cairo will do infinitely more harm to Australia than all the Turks will do in Gallipoli'.[2] The problem was — literally — brought home to Australia when the first soldiers returned from North Africa. By the middle of 1916 it was reported that 'diseased soldiers are being sent to the detention camp at Langwarrin at the rate of 40 a week'.[3] As Vida Goldstein explained to a women's convention called to consider 'the social evil' (a popular euphemism for VD), this situation caused wide-spread alarm:

The war has forced upon us consideration of the question before us. Although the ravages of venereal disease have engaged the attention of certain medical, naval and military men, and a few social workers, for many years past, they have never been forced into the open as they are to-day by the terrible conditions among the soldier. In every belligerent country the naval and military authorities are perturbed as never before; in every belligerent country civilians are aroused as never before and a state of panic is developing...[4]

Meanwhile, however, it had become increasingly clear that professional sex workers were not the real problem. As a Western Australian doctor explained, the 'professional prostitute has her reputation to conserve; a reputation for cleanliness and freedom from disease'.[5] If not prostitutes, who *was* responsible? The doctor was equally confident of the answer: it was the 'amateur prostitute, the street loiterer, the shop girl from 15 to 18'. According to him, these young women were 'often ignorant of the conse-quences of what they do, but they contract disease and spread it...'

The identification of 'the amateur' — a sexually promiscuous, young, working-class woman — as the major culprit in the spread of venereal disease was a new phenomenon, associated directly with wartime conditions. It is difficult to say whether sexual activity among these teenage girls really was such a new occur-rence. Judging by the scandalised comments of contemporaries, it was certainly done much more openly and publicly. Two members of the Women's Political Association, for instance, investigated conditions along St Kilda Road in Melbourne one 'damp, cold night' in May 1916 between 9.30 and 10.00 p.m. They were shocked by what they found.

Every seat along the footpath was occupied by soldiers and girls embracing each other, many of the latter being mere children with short frocks and their hair still hanging down their backs. Some of the girls, apparently overcome by liquor, were almost asleep in their companions' arms. On the grass plots, behind the seats, dozens of men and girls were lying in the dark. They remain there undisturbed all night.[6]

These feminist investigators attributed the lax moral state of affairs directly to the war. The war, they declared, was supposed to be 'a great moral uplifter', but in reality had wrought a 'subtle change in sentiment' resulting in a 'serious decline in sexual morality'. Unlike many of the male commentators, they did not blame only the women, recognising that the sexual act involves at least two parties. A returned soldier, they argued, was often a desperate character. Having endured 'the bodily and mental torture of war', he finds himself 'ruined at the beginning of his life', 'left to shift for himself' by the community for which he has suffered so much. He naturally feels considerable bitterness, which finds expression in a desire to 'get what pleasures he can by riotous behaviour, drink and debauchery'. The investigators also took a sympathetic view of the young women involved in these sexual liaisons:

The girls' point of view is not difficult to enter into, either. The soldiers are held up to them as their protectors, in whom infinite trust can be imposed, and as heroes, to whom nothing can be refused — and also as poor fellows who will so soon be dead, that a tender-hearted, ignorant girl cannot resist granting him what love she has to give.

Responses to this situation varied. There were two broadly different strategies: one relying on voluntarism and social welfare measures; the other resorting to compulsion in an attempt to force people to report and undergo treatment for VD. Even women's groups were divided over the issue. Some, such as Vida Goldstein's Women's Political Association, were totally opposed to any form of compulsory notification and treatment of the disease. They believed that compulsion would lead to evasion of the law because the stigma attached to having a sexually transmitted disease would cause people to conceal their condition for as long as possible. They also feared that compulsory clauses would be applied more often to women than to men, and more often to poorer people than the well-off. It would be, 'in effect, class and sex legislation'.[7] It would be preferable, they argued, to rely on education and other gentle measures aimed at providing a healthier economic and social environment, higher moral standards and safe recreation for the young: 'education, kind treatment and good economic conditions', as one advocate put it.[8] This voluntary approach was directed not just at keeping women from 'the path of sin': it was also directed to transforming Man, to cure his 'moral syphilis', to teach him 'higher ideals of the sex functions' so that he could 'learn to conquer himself' and

Figure 6.1
The Tabbie, or Female Digger (Diggus Feminus)
(*Aussie*, no. 10, January 1919, National Library of Australia)

■ What was Lance Mattinson saying with this sketch?

control his lusts.[9] Women could play a part in this re-education, encouraging men 'not by carping and cavilling' but by a 'quiet insistence', 'by something helpful...in our own influence'. Women delegates to the 1916 conference on the 'social evil' were told of the importance of sending 'kind messages and thoughts' to the soldiers overseas:

A young soldier writing from Egypt said: 'The knowledge that a good woman is praying for him is a wonderful help to a man — a moral antiseptic — and God knows we need it.' He wrote of the 'flaunting haunts of vice where the painted dregs of womanhood look down from the brothel windows.'[10]

Document 6.1

Compulsion versus reconstruction

To the editor

Sir,

The most lamentable thing about the proposals to cope with venereal disease now before Parliament is the fact that the Government is stubbornly attempting to do by compulsion what can only be done by reconstruction. There is ample evidence on every hand to prove that the prevalence and spread of these diseases is very largely due to the economic conditions under which many women and girls live, and we are now in a position to quote from evidence given by two government officials before the Select Committee. Police-woman Dugdale, speaking of one girl in particular, said: 'These girls seem to think that when they have finished with the hospital, they can go back to their old positions. In the case of this girl, when she came out of the hospital, she had no home to go to — she could only go to a room.' There are many girls in Perth who have no homes, and no one seems to care what becomes of them afterwards. 'It is not surprising', the police-woman goes on to say, 'that I afterwards saw this same girl soliciting in the streets.'

Then Sub-Inspector O'Halloran, on the same point says: 'With regard to the question of young girls suffering from venereal disease, the worst feature is that girls who have no means have to get money to live while they are being treated as out-patients at the Perth Public Hospital, and the only means of getting money is by prostitution, and so they are meantime disseminating disease. If there is no room at the hospital, or anywhere else, where they can be kept and treated until cured, then, as far as I can see, it is hopeless to expect these diseases to be eradicated.'

And so we see, Sir, on the evidence of people partially engaged in administering the present Act, that this is how the principle of compulsion is working out for want of adequate facilities. We are being told that the reason the disease is spreading is because there are certain persons known to be diseased whom, under the present Act, the Commissioner cannot get hold of, but here we have it on evidence of people who are in a position to know that those who have been reached by the Health Department, and have in every way surrendered to treatment, are spreading the disease far and wide, through the pressure of want, and there is no suggestion by the Government to remove this great contributing cause. The two officials referred to also gave very pointed evidence on the drink question as being the main cause of discord between husband and wife in the home, which is a fruitful cause of driving young people from their homes.

It is unnecessary to direct the attention of the public to the fact that over and over again the social and religious bodies of the State have pleaded with the Government to deal with:—

1   Proper control of the liquor traffic, especially wine shops (always featuring the protection of the young), and now recognised everywhere as one of the causes of this disease and social degradation.

2   Recognising that the wave of emotion passing over the community, owing to the present crisis, would be a grave cause of danger to young people, the social bodies made repeated requests by deputation to the Government asking for the appointment of 'women patrols' to supervise our parks and public resorts; but two years passed away after the outbreak of war, before two women police were appointed to do this valuable preventative work; and the time is now overdue for their number to be greatly increased.

3 On many occasions the extreme importance of teaching 'social hygiene' to the young has been urged by means of providing suitable courses of lectures to mothers and to our children in schools. The need for the classification of the feeble-minded in our large institutions has been brought under the notice of the powers that be.

4 That every section of the community working for 'child welfare' has urged the Government repeatedly to provide more effective supervision of all 'picture shows' by appointing a State Censor Board; and how many of these requests have received even consideration?

This 'law of the suspect' with which we are threatened has had the effect of causing those people who are most horrified at the suggestion that injustice could be done by it to be themselves the first to amply demonstrate the danger indicated. For instance, we have Dr. Trethowan already specifying classes of women workers amongst whom he expected it to be most prevalent — for instance, the shop girls. And now we have Mr. Lovekin publicly stating that many wives of soldiers are afflicted with this disease. Is it not reasonable to suppose that other staunch supporters of the Bill will discover in due course, say, that typists, lady clerks, teachers, nurses, and other women are causing the most mischief in this way? The very fact that it is being eternally emphasised by some men that women and girls are the main disseminators of this disease should make women hesitate before allowing Parliament to place a law on our Statute Book which allows one man to take action on secret evidence contrary to any court of law. It is high time that the women in the State took the trouble to make themselves more familiar with this class of legislation, humiliating to womanhood as it is, which has always been placed on our Statute Books in the past, and certainly will be again, unless women rise in a body and make our legislators realise that we insist on being treated as individuals and co-equals. Before this Bill is allowed to go through the Lower House, we appeal strongly to women all over the State to join with us in our protest by getting into communication with our secretary, 140 Barrack Street, at once, either personally or by letter.

Yours etc
Bessie Rischbieth,
President,
Women's Service Guild, Perth
(*West Australian,* 13 March 1918)

Although equally concerned about introducing 'sex and class legislation', some politically active women supported compulsion. They hoped legislation compelling diseased people to seek treatment would help prevent men knowingly infecting 'innocent' women. Ultimately, the policies developed during the war showed a combination of these two approaches. Women police were appointed in several states (although, it was lamented, not under the same pay and conditions as men).

One of the greatest 'victories' for women's groups was the early closing of hotels; they hoped this would reduce the incidence of VD by reducing the effect of alcohol on men's (and women's) sexual passions. (Ironically, if six o'clock closing had not become so widespread, those same soldiers who were seen fondling young girls in the streets might have been otherwise occupied in the public bars.) Several states also introduced new health legislation to provide for compulsory notification and treatment of venereal diseases. And young women came under greater surveillance from the authorities, who sometimes removed sexually active teenagers from their families and placed them in institutions where their physical and moral reform was attempted.

■ What does Bessie Rischbieth see as the main cause of the spread of VD?
■ What connection does she see between VD and the 'drink question'? What does she advocate as a solution?
■ Why is she opposed to compulsory notification and treatment of suspects?

Usually these girls were found by the police 'roaming the streets' and 'keeping late hours', often in the company of soldiers and sailors. Others were arrested because it was believed they were responsible for infecting soldiers with venereal disease. These allegations sometimes proved to be false. Fourteen-year-old Daisy L. was sent to a reformatory by a court in 1916. Her file noted that 'she has run away from her home and for three weeks had been leading an immoral life. She admits misconduct with soldiers, two of whom (it is alleged) have since been sent to the Langwarrin VD camp.' After her conviction it was found that she did not have VD but she nevertheless spent fifteen months in a reformatory before being sent home to her mother.[11] Nor was it only the fact that these girls were believed to be infecting servicemen that led to the authorities' concern; the war had increased concern about the future of the 'race', and these young women were supposed to bear and raise healthy children to replace the men killed in battle. It was a heavy burden for

Figure 6.2

(*Punch*, 31 August 1916)

■ How does this cartoon portray women constables, employed for the first time during the war?

Figure 6.3

1918 recruiting poster
(Government Recruiting Poster)

■ Why was this poster entitled 'The Strong Post'?

Australia's womanhood, but one which justified all sorts of government intervention in their lives (both during and after the war) in attempts to make them better mothers. Thus, while the war seemed to offer young women new opportunities for romance and sexual adventure, it also led to more policing of both their public and private lives in the interests of the so-called 'national good'.

Enemy aliens

Fears for 'national security' also determined the treatment of Australia's 'enemy aliens'. The 1911 Census (the last conducted before the outbreak of war) listed almost 35 000 Australian residents who had been born in Germany, Austria and Hungary. In addition, there were entire communities who were descended from early German settlers and who retained, as the official war historian put it, 'a sentimental attachment to the land of their origin'.[12]

In most cases, these German Australians had had no difficulty in reconciling their Australian citizenship with an older cultural inheritance. Before the war, German clubs, newspapers and churches had flourished in many communities, particularly the wine-growing districts of the Barossa and the farms of the Wimmera, Riverina and Darling Downs. These activities were in no way disloyal to the Empire; indeed, when war was declared many such families saw their sons enlist in the Australian armed forces. But the Allied defeats in Gallipoli and France fostered a xenophobic mentality, a fear and suspicion of all things foreign — in this case, all things German. By 1916, 'anything suggestive of German origin was positively toxic to large numbers of worthy citizens'. The music of German composers was banned from leading concert halls and New South Wales state schools considered banning German language classes. German-speaking schools and churches were closely monitored or disbanded and even German place names were altered.[13] In South Australia, Homburg became Haig and Blumberg became Birdwood (the first renamed after a British general and the second after an Australian one). New South Wales changed German Creek to Empire Vale and Victoria dumped Germantown for Grovedale. Tasmania altered Bismark to Collinvale, Western Australia renamed Mueller Park after Kitchener, and Queensland exchanged Hapsburg for Kowbi. The renaming of towns, parks and suburbs was much more than an idle expression of patriotic sentiment; it denied the important contribution of the German-Australians who had 'established' these settlements and repudiated a rich cosmopolitan European culture for one that was narrowly defined as British. Indeed it is interesting that Anglo-Celtic Australians were now prepared to accept Aboriginal place names in preference to those used by the Germans. It was small consolation to those whose lands were taken in a war few people cared to remember.

The fear of all things German also served an immediate political purpose. With the war so far away, it was necessary to imagine a threat much closer to home. For much of the war, the 'sightings' of German submarines, ships and even zeppelins, off Australia's vast and undefended shores was a regular occurrence. Equally credible, it seemed, was the collusion of Australia's thousands of German-speaking people with the forces of the enemy. Clotheslines erected in the rugged Tasmanian ranges were reported as radio masts designed to relay messages to awaiting

■ What do you think the unnamed women and children were thinking as the prisoners of war were marched past them? Why was Mrs Hehir 'wiping tears from her warm and friendly eyes'?

Document 6.2

A young prisoner of war

Anthony Splivalo was born in a village on the Dalmatian coast in 1898. In 1911 he emigrated to the West Australian goldfields. Anthony was imprisoned at the outbreak of war. He was 16 years old.

When all of us had been questioned, Major Corbett rose from his desk and informed us that we would be going to the Rottnest Island camp, leaving that afternoon on the Kalgoorlie–Perth express. His crisp, cold words were like an electric shock. I was stunned. Gaining some composure I walked to Major Corbett to verify whether I, too, was included in the group. 'Yes, everybody!' he replied sourly, without even looking at me. I then asked permission to run home to say goodbye to my Australian family and to my brother, and at the same time to gather enough clothes for one change, at least. He snapped at me with an arrogance not easily forgotten: 'Nobody must leave the hall!' I was terribly frightened, and felt as if in the grip of some monster. What harm had I ever done to anybody?

We waited and waited, like dumb animals, constantly shifting our weight from one foot to another. Uniformed messengers kept coming and going, snapping and saluting…flanked by armed men with cold eyes, we trudged with heavy step down the dusty Brookman Street, silent and wondering what the Gods had decreed for us now.

Thus, just a few months after my seventeenth birthday, I became Western Australia's youngest prisoner of war. My metamorphosis was bewildering. Around me soldiers, rifles, bayonets,

cartridge belts and awful military officiality [sic]. Our guards marched like conquerors; a battle-front air pervaded the situation, as if there had been a skirmish at the top of Hannan Street and we were the captured prisoners. The operation had elements of [a] Gilbert and Sullivan [comic opera].

I marched with my hands stuck into my coat pockets, the Stott College band still around my hat. Men, women and children lined the street to watch us pass. They stood silently, showing no enmity, looking puzzled as if unable to piece things together. I bitterly resented being exposed to public gaze like a criminal under armed guards.

The only sound was that of marching feet. From Brookman Street we turned right into Wilson Street where more people had gathered to watch something never seen before on the goldfields. At the railway station the wide gates opened as if by pre-arrangement, swallowing us and our military guards.

While waiting to entrain I saw, waving to me through the fence, Mrs Hehir, her daughter Vera and my brother Matthew who had come to say goodbye to me. They were barred from the platform. Since I had not returned home that afternoon, the Hehir family and my brother took it for granted that I was on my way into exile. As I waved to them through a row of bristling bayonets, I noticed that Mrs Hehir was wiping tears from her warm and friendly eyes. My heart was heavy too. The picture of this Australian mother weeping for her foreign ward on his way to a prisoner of war camp is deeply etched in my memory. I think this was the most moving moment in my entire Australian experience.

(Anthony Splivalo, *The Home Fires*, Fremantle Arts Press, Fremantle, 1982, pp. 57–8)

German raiders; German sermons in Lutheran churches were thought to be coded with instructions for a German uprising; farmers and orchardists were accused of stockpiling weapons.

Nor were these fears directed only at people of German origin. In the decades prior to the war, large numbers of Slavs had made their way to the mining towns of northern and western Australia. Resented by unions as a potential source of cheap foreign labour, they aroused irrational racial and economic fears which could now take on the 'noble' language of patriotism. The small number of Turkish and Afghan workers in Australia were also readily identified as a nation within a nation, an 'enemy' to loyal British Australia.

The most tangible expression of the fear of 'the enemy within' was the registration, surveillance and, eventually, actual imprisonment of these so-called enemy aliens. The term was always an elastic one. Initially, the definition of 'enemy alien' exempted those who had been naturalised as Australian citizens or were the children of German and Slavic residents who had been born in Australia. But as the war progressed, it extended to include the government's political critics (particularly Irish and American agitators associated with the Industrial Workers of the World) and all those of even remotely German ancestry. Families who had lived in Australia for several generations, successful farmers, prominent businessmen and even politicians, all became suspect. And many were imprisoned. Internment camps were established on islands off the coast of Tasmania and Western Australia and in remote bush settlements in South Australia, New South Wales and Victoria. The camps were often located in disused prisons, although Holdsworthy — the largest, about 40 kilometres from Sydney — was not much more than a maze of hastily erected barbed wire fencing. In concentration camps such as these (this term was used by the authorities) some 6000 inmates saw out the duration (that is, the period of the war). Many were not released until a year after the war had ended, and then forcibly deported to Germany.

Imprisonment was largely a male experience. Fewer than 70 women were imprisoned, and all belonged to 'German' families deported from nearby British colonies in the Asia-Pacific region. Daisy Pearse, a fourth-generation Australian, was born in Fremantle into one of the oldest and most respected families in Western Australia. But Daisy married Alfred Schoeffel, a German. When war broke out, she was living in Fiji with her husband and his cousin and business associate Alfred Kienzle. Both men were long-term residents of Fiji and both had been naturalised as British citizens. But that did not protect them from being summarily deported to Australia for internment with their wives and children. Daisy was sent to the so-called family camp at Bourke in New South Wales. Imprisonment for this Western Australian woman as an 'enemy alien' was a harrowing experience.

Under official surveillance

('Prisoner of War Information: Martha Schunke', Intelligence Section Records, Attorney General's Department, MP 16/1, 1915/3/1635, Australian Archives, Melbourne)

PRISONERS OF WAR INFORMATION
----

1. Surname.   *Schunke née Dowell*
2. Christian Name.   *Martha Helen*
3. Date of Birth.   *10/1/1894*
4. Age.   *21*
5. Place of birth.   *Long Gully, Bendigo*
6. Married, Single, Widower.   *Married*
7. Children, age, sex, etc.   *1 child girl of 4yrs*
8. Address.   *Golden Gully, Bendigo*

9. Resided in Australia.   *all life*
10. If naturalized,
    (Give date, place etc.
    No. of Certificate)
11. Occupation.   *Home duties*
12. References.
13. Naval or Military Service.   *Wishes permission to go*
14. Rank in Army or Navy.   *to Sydney by "Moolton"*
15. If parole is requested.   *on 27th inst.*
        If recommended.
16. Date taken into Custody.
17. Time, place, and by whom.
18. Amount of money taken over
19. Parolled on.   *Husband born in Australia*
20. If can speak English.   *and is at present in camp with*
21. Height.   *A.I.F.*
22. Build.   *Father & mother on husband's side*
23. Hair.   *born in Australia, but grandfather*
24. Eyes.   *was a German.*
25. Complexion.
26. Marks.

--------0000000000--------

app[rove]d
[signature] 26/11/15

■ **Why did the Intelligence Service monitor the movements of Martha Schunke?**

We arrived at Bourke just before dark the next day & were paraded to an empty 2 storeyed brick building, formerly the 'Empire Hotel'. Here the Sergt Major told each family to what room to go to. We had just time to have a glimpse at my room & then darkness set in; there was no light of any kind. When at last I was able to get some candles from a store nearby & [we] were able to see the state of the rooms we had to live in, we women after that hot & long journey just broke down. I wished to God I could die & my babies with me! In my room were two broken bedsteads & nothing else but filth and dirt. This building had been empty for over 2 years. Later on in the evening we were told that there were straw sacks below & if we wanted them to come & get them; there was no other bedding or pillows of any kind. At 10 o'clock that night, we were told that if we wanted anything to eat to come to the kitchen. We were shown a pile of filthy dirty rusty tin plates, a tin mug (dirty). There was some sort of stew rice in a bucket, dirty & greasy, which had previously been used to wash the floor with. Needless to say I had not a taste of food for 24 hours after arriving in Bourke. I politely asked the Sergeant Major could I have a plate to make my baby some food, and he answered 'There's the plates (pointing to the filthy rusty tin ones) that the Australian Government give to the German Prisoners'. I looked him fair in the face & said 'I am neither a German nor a prisoner, but an Australian woman!'. He said 'If you were not a German Prisoner you would not be here!'[14]

Daisy Schoeffel was wrongfully imprisoned in her own country. The same was true of the vast majority of male internees. Recent studies of internment and the home front suggest that very few of these 'enemy aliens' presented any threat to the nation they had adopted as their home. To speak German, to have a German name or (absurd as it may seem) German 'appearance' was enough to warrant suspicion, investigation and sometimes imprisonment. In short, these individuals were different, not dangerous. And imprisonment served personal as well as political motives. What better way of removing a successful business rival than by spreading rumours of his or her sympathies for the enemy?

Figure 6.4
Two families at Bourke Internment Camp, c. 1915
(AWM P0595/174/156)

■ How might you explain the differences between this apparently happy scene and Daisy Schoeffel's account of her experiences as an internee?

Document 6.4

Police surveillance report

(Memo to Captain Jones, Chief of Intelligence Section, 15 July 1915,
Intelligence Section Records, Attorney General's Department, MP 16,
1915/3/980, Australian Archives, Melbourne)

VICTORIA POLICE,—[57.]

INTELLIGENCE SEC'N GENERAL
1915 1 · 3 / 980
3rd. Military District

POLICE DEPARTMENT,

Criminal Investigation Branch.

Melbourne *July 15th* 1915

Subject ... Relative to a complaint made by Mrs Kitz re suspicious men visiting her wine shop in The Royal Arcade off Bourke Street City.

I have to report for your information that Mrs Kitz called at the Detective Office & stated that recently several men have been visiting her Wine Shop at the above mentioned address, whose manner she thought are suspicious, that sometimes they speak in the German language & she has heard them say 'The Government has chartered 11 boats & they must buy it.' She described the men as follows.

1st) Thinks his name is Kantu short, thick set, clean shaven, fair complex, clea large stomach, dresses fairly well generally in grey, soft felt hat, & about 47 to 50 years of age.

2nd) Proprietor of Boundary Hotel, clean shaven, pale face, wears diamond ring on left small finger, always wears coat with large cape & is always addressed as Captain.

3rd) 45 years of age, fair hair, black moustache, hard face, generally wears rain coat, said to be very smart.

4th) Draughtsman, about 5ft 11in has grey & black hair, dark overcoat, boxer hat.

Captain Jones
Chief of
Intelligence Section

F W Biddick
Const 5653

■ What is it about these men which makes Mrs Kitz suspicious?

Hunting 'the Hun' at home also provided an emotional outlet for those who could not take any direct part in the hostilities in Europe. Readers of the Sydney *Mirror* thrilled to stories of Germans still 'at large' in the city. Among these 'enemy aliens' was Edmund Resch, the brewer, and the shipping agent Oscar Plate, whose home at Elizabeth Bay (suspiciously!) overlooked the naval dockyards of Garden Island. Patriotic women, many of whom had menfolk serving abroad, believed the anti-German campaign was a practical way of helping them or even avenging the lives of loved ones lost in Europe. An Anti-German Women's League was founded by the same sort of women who publicly advocated compulsory military service. In 1917, its officers wrote to the Prime Minister, pledging their support 'for the destruction of the enemy' and alleging there were 'at least 148 employees with foreign names' in key positions in the public service.[15]

Document 6.5

'Hun' women

Two Sydney cases

(Special to 'The Mirror')

Mention has been made in our pages more than once of Hun women who are a danger to the community.

One of the worst examples of these, owing to her position in society, is Frau J. F. Utz, of 'Stuttgart', Wright Road, Drummoyne. She is a full-blooded Hun, the wife of a Hun storekeeper who made his money in the country, and is now endeavouring to force her way into Sydney society.

She has more than one son. One of these recently had the impudence to try and pass the Officers' School, with a view of going away with the A.I.F. Luckily his parentage was discovered and it was intimated to him that his room would be preferable to his company.

Another son is still a schoolboy, who is in receipt, under his Hun father's will, of £10 a week, and it is understood that when he comes of age he will, as Kipling puts it, come into 'awful opulence' of his own.

* * *

Another Hun woman whom the authorities apparently allow to remain at large to her own huge delight and to the annoyance of her neighbours is Frau Engert, of Coogee. This Hun woman has resided in the locality for many years, and even at the present time is never tired of boasting of the fact that there is only one nation on the face of the earth, and that is her own. She has a husband who was naturalised some twenty years ago — probably for the usual Hun diplomatic purposes — and the husband has recently been allowed to return to his connubial joys from some other country — whether the Fatherland or not he does not say. Both of these Huns might be very well placed where they can do no harm, and where the female one at least cannot annoy tram passengers on the Coogee line by her German presence and remarks.

(Mirror, 15 January 1916, p. 2)

■ What threat did Frau Utz and Frau Engert pose to Australia's national security? Was the *Mirror*'s report racist?

■ What does this case tell us about the plight of German–Australian families who were *not* interned? Who could this family turn to for help?

Document 6.6

Nationality against him

Mrs F. (No. 52) — Husband (German settler) was a fitter, able to earn £3 weekly; out of work for months. Children, six (14, 12, 10, 9, 7, 2). Rooms occupied, five. Earnings: Wife, 8/–.

Spend weekly	s.	d.
Rent	13	0
Bread	3	0
Meat	1	6
Milk	4	0
Butter	1	0
Cheese	0	6
Eggs	1	0
Sugar	0	9
Tea	0	9
Oatmeal	0	3
Sago	0	3
Flour	0	6
Soap	0	1
Kerosene	1	0
Blacking	0	3
Vegetables	1	6
Wood	0	6
School materials	1	0
Church (children)	0	6
Medicine	1	0
Total	**£1** **8**	**10**

This family has been living on past savings, now all exhausted; husband earns a little: nationality against him, although naturalised and has lived in Australia for many years: wife Australian. Children and parents have been without food for days at a time: mother very tidy and clean, baby coming.
(*Woman Voter*, 24 February 1916)

For targeted men, the costs of this campaign were obvious — dismissal from employment, isolation, harassment, even imprisonment. But attacking 'the enemy' had an equally catastrophic effect on 'the enemy's' family.

As noted earlier, only women and children from British colonies were actually imprisoned. Economics and not security was the principal consideration here. The British Government (or the colonies concerned) paid for the maintenance of such families in prison. The Australian Government was not so 'generous' when it came to maintaining the families of its own 'enemy aliens'. With the husband interned, wives and children were often left to fend for themselves; the only assistance offered was an (unreliable) payment of 10s per week to the wives of (some) voluntary internees and 2s 6d for every child under the age of 14. Moved by the suffering of Slav families in the mining towns, the Archbishop of Perth described this as a 'starvation allowance'.

Document 6.7

German internees complain

The following petition was sent to the German Government in early 1918.

Writing on behalf of married German internees, whose wives and families are resident in Australia, we beg to ask our [German] Government to take such steps which will effectively prevent the unnecessarily severe and injurious treatment to which our families and ourselves are subjected by the Australian Government...

In support of our requests, we beg to state:

a   that most of the undersigned have now been interned for about two years, and some for three years;

b   that only a small percentage of the internees in question are enabled to see their families once a week for a few hours, under none too favourable conditions. This small percentage comprises those whose families live in or near Sydney, and those very few others who can afford to transfer their families from other States to Sydney and maintain them there;

c   that the remainder of the section in question have not seen their wives nor families since they were brought to this internment Camp [Holdsworthy];

d   that the end of the war is as remote as ever, and, in the absence of releasing internees on parole, their captivity may yet last for years;

e   that great economical, mental, physical hardships have been thrown upon the wives of internees by reason of their husbands' internment. The businesses or farms of their families are in ruins, the breadwinners of the families forcibly removed and, in the majority of cases, deported to another State. Their savings gone, internees' families are now mostly existing under very distressing circumstances. In some cases, internees' wives or members of internees' families are cripples or helpless invalids, unable to earn money. In other cases, families are large, including helpless little children, and the separation allowances are hopelessly inadequate to sustain them. As a rule, women, who are known to be married to internees, and their children, are persecuted and hunted by hostile sections of the community in which they live. In more than one case, the wives of the internees have lost their reason, and in many cases, the health of internees' wives has completely broken down. And in all cases the miseries of their families react upon the husbands, and cause them mental agonies, which in one instance already ended in the mind of the unfortunate becoming unbalanced and [him] committing suicide. It must also be borne in mind that some of us came into the Camp unable to find work and under the promise given by responsible internment officers that their families would be paid sufficient allowance, and that they could regain their liberty whenever work should be offered them and, now find that these promises are not kept and [they] are detained against their will;

f   that this long sustained imprisonment, unlimited as to time...possesses the inherent danger of estranging wives from their husbands, and children from their fathers, which, in the case of Australian women married to internees of enemy origin, is accentuated by the mind-poisoning press campaign against everything of enemy origin. In some cases, wives of internees have already demanded separation from their husbands, and in others irrevocable estrangement has taken place between them, and in all cases intense sufferings are being endured;

g   most of us have an honorable and clean record as residents of Australia, and have been useful and peaceful citizens. The prospect of being deprived of our liberty for years under conditions involving such wrecking of homes, health and happiness is unbearable. But quite apart from any contentions, we maintain that we and our families are entitled to the humane treatment which is in the power and which is the moral obligation of a civilised and wealthy country to give to its internees irrespective of the expense incurred thereby. The saving, if any, effected by the Government under the prevailing cruel treatment of internees and their families is made only at our expense and by punishing innocent women and children.

(Report for the Imperial German Government re Complaint of Married German Internees with Families in Australia, 28 January 1918, MP 367/1, 567/10/189, Australian Archives, Melbourne)

■   What insight does this petition give us into the plight of the families of 'enemy aliens' during the war?

■   Do you think their treatment was justified? Explain your response.

And women left alone had no one to protect them from the harassment of patriotic citizens. In October 1916, Mrs Grete Halfeke found herself just as much a prisoner as her husband out at Holdsworthy:

We have…been living in a room and the children are continually getting sick, and I am unable to care for them through fright, I am in fear of going out or letting the children out, as they have often been attacked by a woman in the neighbourhood, who has also threatened myself with violence.

Some time ago stones have been thrown through my window at night, and since that I have been unable to sleep, and my nerves are getting so bad that I am afraid something terrible will happen [to] myself and my children as I feel the strain is too much for one to bear much longer…[16]

At least Mrs Halfeke had a roof above her head. Another mother, Lotte Hahn, appealed to the Governor-General to heed the plight of her innocent children:

Being an Alien Subject and in deep trouble, I am writing asking your help and protection. My landlord has given me notice to leave the cottage with my three little children, because I am a German. The prejudice here is so bitter that I cannot send my two little boys to school. I am utterly unnerved through worry and anxiety… My husband [Richard Hahn] has been interned at Liverpool two years and my baby girl was born eighteen months ago. My funds are almost out. I implore you to help me in this matter as soon as possible, as I do not know where to get a roof to cover our heads.[17]

Both women requested that they and their families be interned with their husbands. At least in prison they might have a chance of protecting and educating their children. Both requests, and innumerable others, were dismissed out of hand. Not long after, the Governor-General and his wife, Lady Munro Ferguson, attended yet another function to benefit Australian children orphaned by the war. Apparently, Christian charity did not extend to the children of the 'enemy'.

The war had left a scar on a new generation of Australians. And it was not just the children of 'enemy aliens' who would suffer in its aftermath.

Suggestions for study

To discuss

1   Form groups of about seven. Each group represents a military committee charged with organising internal security in a district of Australia during the war. What measures do they decide to take?

2   The government has proposed changes to the Health Act whereby it will be compulsory for doctors to inform the authorities of patients suffering from venereal diseases. Convene a public meeting to discuss this. At the meeting, there are

representatives of the medical profession, the Women's Peace Army, the women's committee of the Australian Labor Party, the Australian Women's National League and many returned soldiers. Each group is to put its opinion on the merits of the proposal.

To write about

1   Tony Splivalo, a Kalgoorlie teenager, corresponded with several of his school friends after he was interned as an enemy alien. Reconstruct an exchange of letters between one of these friends and Splivalo. One of Splivalo's letters is written from Rottnest Island, the other from Holdsworthy, near Sydney.

2   You are the Australian wife of a German-born husband. Write to the authorities putting the case against his deportation at the end of the Great War.

3   It is 1916 and there has been much discussion in parliament and the press about the sudden upsurge in the incidence of venereal disease. Many of the commentators blame 'young shopgirls'. You are an 18-year-old shop assistant. Write a letter to the editor of a newspaper putting your point of view.

To research

1   Using your local community history resources, find out if any of the names of streets, towns or suburbs in your area were changed during the Great War.

2   Draw up a table of the ethnic background of your class members. Would any of the class members, or their parents, have been liable for internment during the Great War?

CONCLUSION: THE AFTERMATH

7

War ended in Europe on 11 November 1918. But the aftermath of war was felt long after the killing was over. Australia had mobilised an army of some 400 000 men, an enormous effort for a country of just under 5 million people. Of these, 330 000 had been sent abroad and over 68 per cent became casualties (60 000 died). It was the highest casualty rate of any of the Allied armies; it literally crippled a young and promising nation.

Figure 7.1

Making the best of an enforced stay at Portsea Quarantine Station, 1919 (AWM P1425/17)

■ Why were returning nurses and soldiers forced to stay here?

Australia after the war was a country of widows. The emotional cost of war was terrible enough; women as we have seen, mourned for men who had promised companionship for a lifetime. But there were also practical considerations. In an age which defined men as providers and women as their dependants, over 8000 women were left without a breadwinner and many more thousands of children were orphaned. The war may have killed men far from home; it also wreaked havoc on the families they left behind them.

Australia had pioneered welfare legislation in the late nineteenth and early twentieth centuries so it was not surprising that it was one of the first countries to provide pensions to the widows of servicemen. The allowance was modest enough. After intense lobbying by returned servicemen, a payment was set at around a quarter of the basic male wage, barely enough to keep a family at subsistence level. And if the government pension was inadequate, private schemes offered only qualified relief to the needy. The South Australian Soldiers' Fund was one of several charitable organisations established to care for families 'when the news of the death of the soldier came to hand'. The administrators of the Fund were empowered to assess all applications for assistance and withhold money from widows deemed to be of 'dissolute, immoral or extravagant habits'. Charitable bodies had long made a distinction between the 'deserving' and the 'undeserving' poor; the wives of the nation's 'dead heroes' were not to be treated any more kindly. Applicants for assistance were obliged to divulge details of their personal lives, lest they be considered 'unworthy'; and even the smallest items of expenditure were scrutinised by an all-male committee headed by a Mr Winterbottom. In the *Diggers' Gazette* (published by a forerunner of the RSL), one returned soldier protested:

They are…put through an inquisition that is nothing short of scandalous. They must detail what each penny is to be spent on. One widow informed me that she asked for a grant for clothing. The inquisitor asked, 'What clothing?' She replied, 'Mostly underclothing.' But this answer was not sufficient — she must needs detail every item of her underwear. One of the items was a pair of silk stockings. She was told to wear cotton… I am giving this instance to show the humiliating position these defenceless women are put in by men who would hesitate to cross-examine their own wives in the same manner, but who think the soldier's widow 'fair game' for their insolence… Most of the women who have been refused are good women and good mothers, and some of them are desperately in need of the money for actual necessities.[1]

The South Australian Soldiers' Fund may not have been fair; it could well be argued that the entire welfare system set up around repatriation wasn't fair either. Women whose husbands were killed in battle were entitled to a pension; women whose husbands were killed making the guns they fought with were not. A sick soldier was entitled to attend one of the hundreds of repatriation hospitals set up throughout the country; those who were injured at work

Document 7.1

'Read these pathetic letters...'

(*Diggers' Gazette*, 15 November 1919)

Read these Pathetic Letters from Widows of your Fallen Comrades.

TOLD TO GO OUT AND WORK.

"I have been a widow for nearly four years, and have one little girl. I was granted £75 from the Insurance Fund, but the money was not to be paid into my account. If I wanted any of it, I had to apply for it and state what I wanted it for. I was given no explanation why it was not paid to me. As I am neither extravagant and have always lived a pure life, I don't know what excuse they had for not doing so. I went in later to ask for a portion of it, as I wanted my verandah closed in one end . . . also some blankets and house linen . . . and was granted £17 10/ after going in several times and waiting half the day. For nearly three years I had only 30/ a week, and my clothes and house linen got down. I was not able to replace them, and I have never been able to go out and work and earn anything, as I was told to do when I went to the Soldiers' Fund on one occasion. My little girl has been very delicate, and is still far from strong. I think it is hard enough to give our husbands without having to have our babies looked after by other people, as they must be if we have to work. I am not complaining about the money we get now, as I think we are getting a very fair thing, and can manage very well if we are careful but I do think it was very unfair to pay some the whole amount and not others."

PATHETIC PETITION IGNORED.

"I had to go and almost beg for help for clothing for three of my daughters, who are ill with consumption. . . . Well, in the end, they gave me £6 in order for clothing, and I had to divide that between three girls. . . . I wrote to the Chairman of the Insurance Committee . . . but so far they have not answered my letter."

DOLED OUT LIKE CHARITY—AND RELUCTANT CHARITY AT THAT.

"Some time ago I went and saw Mr. Winter-Bottom, and he said the money was set aside for the benefit of the children. However, three months ago I saw him again. He gave me £5 for one of them. He told me to come again in three months' time for another £5. When I went on Tuesday, Mr. Nancarrow said there was nothing there for me, and to come again in a fortnight's time. I never heard anything about getting anything for the other two children. Hoping to hear from you soon, as I am in need of the money."

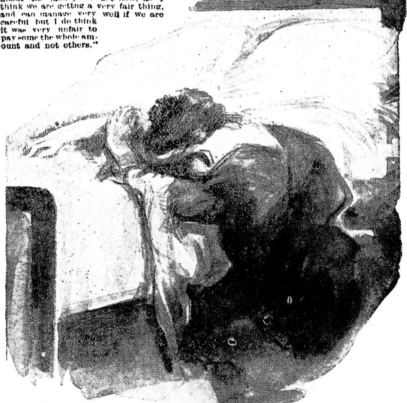

In the Gethsemane of her saddened home the lonely Widow is compelled to drain the bitter cup to its last dreg.

■ Why did the *Digger's Gazette* champion the cause of these women?

■ Why were some women denied assistance by a charitable body set up on their behalf?

■ Do you think the Fund would have operated more fairly if it had been a government-controlled body?

sites or who fell ill with the exhaustion of raising young families had no access to such medical treatment. The war thus created a new inequality in Australian society. The sick, the needy, the widowed were divided into two separate groups — those whose problems were seen as 'war-related' and those whose troubles were their own — and often it was officials like Mr. Winterbottom who distinguished between the two. Nor were returned soldiers *automatically* entitled to government help. They had to *prove* that their injuries were the direct result of service overseas. By the 1930s, it was apparent that the life expectancy for returned soldiers was several years less than the rest of the population. Many of these men received no compensation whatever.

Whatever assistance they might receive from the State, the care of those who did return lay largely with women. Throughout the war, wives and mothers had been told that their men fought heroically: Australia's soldiers, in the poet John Masefield's oft-quoted phrase 'walked like princes [and] looked like kings'. By war's end, many did not walk at all. Maimed men hobbled off the hospital ships on their crutches or were wheeled off in chairs and beds. The young and strong were blinded, paralysed and disfigured. Thousands coughed compulsively, their lungs slowly corroding from the effects of poisoned gas. By 1920, 22 742 veterans had been hospitalised; over 68 000 managed as best they could on their disabilities pension.

George Johnston's parents were both involved in the war. His father fought at Gallipoli and in France. His mother became a VAD 'nurse' in a Melbourne military hospital and took home many lonely disabled men to nurse back to complete health after they were discharged. Johnston drew upon his childhood memories of these men in his famous novel *My Brother Jack*:

Some stayed a few weeks or a few months, there were others who were with us for years. Altogether I suppose forty or fifty of them must have inhabited our house at one time or another… [There was] Aleck, who had been blinded early, at Gaba Tepe, with his polished leggings and his Boy Scoutish hat with the four dents in it: and 'Stubby', who was really only a trunk and a jovial red face in a wheel-chair, a German whizzbang having taken both his legs and both forearms at Villers-Bretonneux… Then there was Bert, the gawky, tow-headed Australian country boy who had been a real 'hayseed' when he had volunteered. He had been under age then and had given a false name, but after all that he lost his right leg on the first and only day of action he ever saw in France… The night-marish one in this remembered gallery is Gabby Dixon, because he kept in the background and was never seen much, and I don't suppose he wanted to be seen because he had suffered terrible facial burns with mustard gas and his face was no longer really like a face at all. He used to frighten me with his staring silences…sometimes at night through the thin partitions of the wall we could hear him sobbing in his room.[2]

And men who went to war were scarred in other ways as well. The most unnerving were the 'shell shock' cases, men driven hysterical by the terror of battle and the ceaseless roar of the guns.

WHO SPILT THAT CIGARETTE - ASH ?

Figure 7.2
(*Remnants from Randwick* [pamphlet issued by patients at the Randwick Military Hospital], Randwick, c. 1918, National Library of Australia)

■ What does this patient's sketch suggest about the relationship between hospitalised returned soldiers and their carers?

The symptoms often defied any treatment. Men twitched compulsively, stared blankly into space or cried like children through night and day. In almost every Australian home, the horror of war intruded. Men became strangers to wives and children who lived in a world they had left behind them; loving husbands became paranoid and violent; strong and able men broke down in tears. Then there was what doctors came to diagnose as 'the burnt-out soldier' — the man who was depressed, listless, unable to hold down a job, tired at the beginning of every day. This was the legacy of war to Australian women; these were the wounds they could never heal.

Document 7.2

'I've had no life...'

Mrs Bosco ran the haberdashery business three doors down. She was a woman whom Life didn't like. Her husband had a silver plate in his head — his kiss-me-foot from Gallipoli, she called it — and when he wasn't having a fit, he often sat out in the sunshine on the back steps and quietly sobbed for hours on end. As well as Mr Bosco, Mrs Bosco looked after her aged father, who, inexplicably, always walked backwards...

The haberdashery shop did not provide a living income, and the little woman, prematurely withered, always with bits of cotton in her hair, made corsets for one of the big stores in the city. My father called her a harness-maker, and my mother said, 'Oh, you be quiet, what do you know!' very annoyed.

The shop for which Mrs Bosco did piecework sent her boxes of lolly pink coutil, accompanied by blueprints, and she sewed the bits together on her heavy duty machine, which I often heard roaring away in the middle of the night. The thick coutil upset me a good deal more than Mr Bosco did; it was terrible to think that I might some day have to wear something like that myself.

Mr Bosco, getting worse, began shouting in the night. Once I came into our kitchen to find his wife sitting there, painful tears oozing from her tired eyes, slow as syrup.

'I can't bring myself to put him away, Mrs Park', she said. 'When he's all right he begs me not to. Oh, God, why do men have to go to war?'

She had looked after him for seventeen years, and the almost senile old father for ten.

'I've had no life, Mrs Park', she said. 'I don't suppose I should complain about it, but that's the truth. Charlie joined up only six weeks after we married. No, I've had no life. None.'

(Ruth Park, *A Fence Around the Cuckoo*, Viking, Ringwood, 1992, pp. 123–4)

■ In both Australia and New Zealand, women were left to care for the broken minds and bodies of the Anzacs. What does this care entail for Mrs Bosco? How well does she cope with her burdens?

It was not just wounds that the soldiers brought back with them. As the war drew to a close, a new form of influenza claimed over a hundred thousand lives in Europe. Australian soldiers were among its victims, many dying as their ships drew within sight of their homeland. There was no cure for the 'Spanish flu', so elaborate measures were necessary to contain the spread of the pandemic. The Australian public had been spared many of the hardships of war. Ironically, now that the war was over, their schools, churches and theatres were closed and they were required to wear masks in public places. By 1921, the flu had claimed over 12 000 victims, with women and children proving the most vulnerable to the virus. Almost twice the number of Australians died of the flu as those who 'fell' at Gallipoli, and it killed about 20 million people worldwide. But death by influenza is not the stuff of legends.

Figure 7.3

VADs with face masks during influenza epidemic
(AWM P1102/40/21)

■ **Why were nurses so at risk?**

Venereal disease also came home with the soldiers. With each shipload of wounded came a number of diseased men; often they were marched onto the wharf by a separate gangway, lest awaiting crowds cheer their arrival (VD victims were dishonourably discharged from the services). But once discharged, these men were free to mingle with the civilian population. Venereal disease had been difficult enough to contain in wartime. As the peace grew nearer, Mrs Edgeworth David presided over the formation of a national movement 'to improve the moral tone and physical well being of the people'. Among its principal aims was the issue of a compulsory certificate for couples who wished to wed — a 'guarantee [to] the contracting parties' of 'a clean marriage'. 'No man willing to infect a woman with a loathsome disease can possibly love her', Mrs Edgeworth David declared, 'and vice versa.' But the movement did little to protect Australian women. In the years following the war there was a dramatic increase in the incidence of venereal disease — even in what Mrs Edgeworth David would have called 'respectable' families.[3]

Some of the diggers' sexual liaisons ended in disease; others ended in marriage. The war brides of the Second World War are a popular memory; thousands of young women left Australia to marry foreign (mostly American) servicemen. In the First World War the traffic was in the opposite direction. By 1920, about 14 000 wives and fiancées had left England and France for a new life in

Australia. It could not have been easy. As early as 1917, public criticism was directed at the 50 soldiers a week marrying in 'the old country':

Of course, there is nothing to prevent Bill or Jim from marrying a Chinese peach if he wants to but he will scarcely be given a glad eye by the local lassies on his return. English roses are said to be good, if you pick a goodun, but why the rose when the wattle blossoms bloom in the golden light of this sun-kissed country?[4]

There were no glad eyes for the servicemen's brides either. English women were considered 'loose' by many Australians; how else could they have lured the men away from fiancées and sweethearts they had left behind? Women from the Continent were even more suspect. They were 'foreigners' in ways British women were not; they spoke differently, dressed differently and drank far too much coffee!

■ Why does Jeanne find it so difficult to adjust to her new life in Australia?

■ Are Australians 'the friendliest people under the sun'?

Document 7.3

Jeanne, a war bride

Jeanne, the French wife of returned soldier Jim Davidson, is talking to her husband's lifelong friend Cliff. It is ten years since she arrived as a bride in Australia.

CLIFF: How're things?
          [JEANNE *answers with an expressive glance.*]
          Like that, is it?
JEANNE: Horrible! Much worse than I ever could have thought.
CLIFF: Jim lost many sheep?
JEANNE: Many. Every day I hope that no more sheep will die but every morning when I look out of that door there I can see them lying on the ground, too weak to get up. And the crows…
          [*She shudders.*]
          How did God ever come to make such dreadful creatures as those crows?
CLIFF: I know.
          [*A silence while they both smoke.*]
JEANNE: [*looking at the door*] It is hard to believe that there ever was grass on those plains. Not a blade, not a leaf.
CLIFF: Yet, when the rain comes, you'll see them turning green again. It seems to happen right before your eyes and all your sheep will start to fatten up.
JEANNE: The rain! Is it ever going to come in time? When I have shivered in the snow and sleet in Paris, I never thought that I would come to hate the sun as I do now.
CLIFF: Sunny Australia, eh?
JEANNE: How long do you think this drought can last?
CLIFF: That's hard to say. It could go on for months, it could begin to rain next week.
JEANNE: There are times when I feel it is not going to rain till everything is lost, everything is ruined. Then, when it is too late, God will laugh at us — and send His rain.

CLIFF: Hi! That's no way to talk. What put that into your head?

JEANNE: One by one, all the things that we have hoped for have been taken from us. Why not everything?

CLIFF: That's a lot of nonsense, and you know it.

JEANNE: I have not been very lucky for the Davidsons. Sometimes, I think my coming here was all a big mistake.

CLIFF: What gives you that idea? Has Jim ever said it?

JEANNE: Jim? No, never.

CLIFF: Who has, then? His mother?
            [*She nods her head.*]
            Surely you're not going to let that spiteful old devil come between you and Jim? That's all she's after. Don't let her pull it off.

JEANNE: It is not only her.

CLIFF: Who else has been bothering you?

JEANNE: [*passionately*] Why does no one like me? Why does no one treat me like an ordinary woman? Everybody seems to think because I am French that I am different. Not nice. Not the kind of woman they could make a friend of.

CLIFF: Nonsense.

JEANNE: Nonsense is it! I know I make mistakes when first I come, I take the hand of some, make jokes that no one understand. I smile at some I do not know, some man perhaps, but what is that? Not enough to treat me as they do.

CLIFF: How do they treat you, Jeanne?

JEANNE: Like as if I am…bad woman.

CLIFF: You're just being silly. You're imagining all this.

JEANNE: Imagining? Not I! Sometimes, I feel so lonely I could die. When I come here I want to be the friend of everyone. I try, I try, but no one seem to understand. I tell you, Cliff, that there is no one — *no one* — here but you that I can talk to.

CLIFF: [*suddenly serious*] Listen, Jeanne, you've got the wrong idea. We Australians are the friendliest people under the sun. Somehow, you've got off on the wrong foot.

JEANNE: Have I? What foot is right foot, can you tell me? Is there any right foot here for someone who is not Australian?

(Betty Roland, *The Touch of Silk*, Currency Press, Sydney, 1988 [1955], pp. 44–6)

It is not surprising that many Australian women came to fear and resent these newcomers to their country. Finding a husband in the years after the war was far from easy. The war had depleted the marriageable stock of men — thousands had been killed and thousands more crippled. Australia became not just a nation of widows but also a nation of 'spinsters'. Folklore has it that in one street alone in Geelong, every woman of marriageable age had lost a fiancé; the vast majority of these women never married.

The men who returned had been promised 'a land fit for heroes'. That made the disappointment of repatriation all the more

Figure 7.4

Beatrice Roe weds 2nd Lieutenant Mervyn Cummings, MM (formerly No. 5 Squadron, Australian Flying Corps), in Hobart, 1920.
(AWM P1432/04)

■ Lieut. Cummings received the Military Medal for bravery in battle. How do you think he would have adjusted to a quiet married life in Hobart?

■ As this diary extract implies, not all the children of the diggers were conceived in marriage. Who cared for this digger's baby on the voyage to Australia? Who do you think would have raised the child in Australia?

Document 7.4

'Aftermaths'

24 August 1919 [Tilbury dock, England]: Miss C. came down to say goodbye & a bombshell about an infant which an AIF father is taking out [home] & of course the Sisters are to be saddled with it — but he's anxious 'to do the right thing'! A bit late in the day. Perhaps it's evidence for a divorce.

26 August: Patients came on board during the day — also the Sutton Veny nurses & the Infant — a great deal of worry over it. However 2 of the girls volunteered to look after it: the 'sentiment' & 'womanly feeling' being worked to the uttermost. Australia must have plenty of money. If the men had only known a year or so ago what Australia can do, we'd have had thousands of 'Aftermaths' to take home.

(Diary of Sister Alice Kitchen, Ms 9627, La Trobe Library, Melbourne) hard to take. Barely a decade after the Great War had ended, the Great Depression began. Thousands were thrown out of work, men left their families for uncertain lives on the track, or stayed idle at home, watching those they loved slowly starve. Women like Jean Hayes who had coped with the wreckage of war, now coped with the wreckage of unemployment as well:

My husband was awarded a Military Medal for bravery. I often wondered what our two boys thought of that when they saw him sitting with his head in his hand, too scared to go out again to try for yet another job when he'd been knocked back for years of trying. Humiliated, ashamed in front of his own sons.

For the first few months he used to be just angry, then he was violent, but after that time he just…he cried sometimes. If he cried in front of the boys he took it out on all of us, me and the kids. He was ashamed of not being a proper man with a job. That's the way he saw it. He was so angry with the world he had to take it out on someone, and we were nearest him, so we copped it. I understood and I think the boys did too, although they left home young and went to the country and enlisted from there in 1939.[5]

Jean's husband lived in the city but life was just as hard for returned soldiers who tried to make a living off the land. Alarmed by the number of men returning from the war with no jobs to go to, state governments across Australia instituted soldier settlement schemes. Men (and their families) were settled on marginal (often poor) land, many with no experience of farming, and thousands hampered by injuries sustained during the war. A farm of one's own was intended to instil the manly virtues of thrift, hard work and independence; building on the disciplines the soldier had learnt at war. Instead men fell deeper into debt and dependence, each crop taken by the government (in debt repayment) even before it was harvested from the ground. Years of seemingly point-less toil broke the spirit of even the bravest soldiers. And it broke up their families as well.

Ethel Lester lasted just a few years on their dairying block at Mia Mia, Victoria. There was the endless slog of feeding cattle, clearing land and milking cows — a woman's hard physical labour was essential to keep the property going — and it was hard bringing up children in a shanty on the fringes of the bush. Ethel's husband struggled with a violent sense of failure and shame:

I [Ethel] helped in all kind of manual work milking cows 26 at one stage for just the two of us to manage, rabbiting to get a few shillings to get clothes for self and children and…bed linen or necessities for house apart from food… One day I helped to hold fencing wire to thread through posts — unfortunately I got a 'kink' in the wire which touched a vital spot and before I knew where I was my husband threw me down by catching hold of my throat with his muddy hands. A gentleman called and the first thing — 'oh get a cup of tea' — I wonder did he think of his cruel marks which were left when I gave out the cups of tea.[6]

Ethel left her husband in 1930, taking her children with her. In all, about half the soldier settlers walked off their land, leaving behind years of thankless labour and shattered hopes and dreams.

Document 7.5

'I do not wish to leave as a beggar'

Women as well as men became 'soldier settlers'. Most were soldiers'
widows but some, like Annie Smith, had served overseas, nursing. 'Sister
Smith' (as the locals continued to call her) settled on a dairy farm near
Thorpdale, Victoria, in 1920 but was forced off six years later.

(Letter from Annie Smith to Closer Settlement Board, 18 August 1926,
VPRS 10381, DSL 1605, Public Records Office of Victoria. We thank Marilyn
Lake for drawing our attention to this source.)

Urgent   Walpoles 131 A
                      Thorpdale
                        18/8/26

%o
The Closer Settlement Bd

Dear Sirs

      When Mr O'Keefe
(Farm Supervisor) called
to see me there were
several items I omitted
to mention to him. i.e
that I had put my
War Gratuity amounting
with 4 Years Interest to
£118 into the place, also
my pension money.

Acknowledged also that my record
A   in Comparison with at
19/8/26   least half a dozen soldiers
              who have left their
              blocks in the Vicinity
              was I should say
              favorable, as for one
              thing alone, none of
              my Stock has died

and I have not disposed
of any of the Boards property
without permission.

In regard to my indebtedness
On June 25th 1926 I received
my a/c for liabilities
Total £ 492 – 6 – 4
but when I spoke of a
possible buyer, an account
came in on August 11th
stating liabilities as
Total arrears £ 933 – 6 – 9
Can you explain discrepancy.
I am in this position
that if I were to go off the
place of my own accord I
wd. be penniless, having
put all I possessed into the
improvement of the place
& naturally going off like
that does not appeal to
me. I do not wish to leave
as a beggar.
Again in regard to my liabilities

When I came on to this
place it was one large
paddock. Had not been
cultivated for many years.
I think sheep had been grazed
on it. The paddocks now under
cultivation, were then the
roughest portion. One that is
now perfectly clean. It was covered
with bracken as tall as myself,
with sword grass & hazel clumps,
another with bracken & gorse
most of these cleared by myself &
the the land outside the place kept
clean by me. All subdivided
fences have been put up
in my time here. In addition
to fencing supplied by Board
I have supplied 200 post & 150
droppers, 10 coils barbed wire,
also tie wire, nails & staples &
paid labor for all. There is
still the same amount of
stock here as on the

beginning. The tanks are
in good order also spouting,
separator in good order & implements
not much the worse for wear
so anyone else taking over
ud get a remarkably good
start, with a new fences, 8
paddocks 5 of these sown
with oat & with grasses
+ clovers. In addition to grass
seed supplied my Board I have
bought 1 bus cocksfoot, 2 lb S. clover
25 lb rye grass seed.

There have been innumerable small
things to set in order, pig styes, cow bails
flooring, piping, leak sheds, fencing 7/ place
for stack, water troughs +c +c.

Pardon gentlemen my writing
thus at length, & me if I ask
your consideration. Do you
not think that a little or
this £1000 000 that a little
is being written of Soldiers debts
might also be devoted to my
interest. Yours faithfully
(Mrs) A.M. Smith

■ Would Annie Smith's situation have been any different had she
been a man? How?

Ethel Lester escaped a violent husband with not much more than her children and a few turkeys she 'stole' from the farm. For her, the war (and its aftermath) was an unmitigated tragedy. But the long-term effects of the Great War on Australian women are much more difficult to assess; particularly when we survey each of the groups we've encountered in this study.

For those nurses who went abroad, war experience could prove an advantage. Most found ready employment in the hospital industry which sprang up around repatriation, and appointments as matrons in Red Cross homes were offered to Army nursing sisters. The war enhanced career prospects. Laura Grubb, for instance, used part of her severance pay to finance further training in midwifery. She was then well equipped to take up a position as matron of a country hospital in Western Australia. But while Army nurses received preferential employment, pensions and entitlements, those who had worked for the Red Cross received no official acknowledgement whatever for their services. For these women, the war left a bitter memory. Restless, depressed and confused, few settled back easily into the civilian life they had left behind them.

It was hard, too, for those who had lost their loved ones at war to put their lives back together (grief, as we have seen, cast a dark cloud over a generation of Australians) but widowhood did have its compensations. An inadequate pension was better than none at all, particularly at a time when most widowed women were at the tender mercy of private charity. And widows could take up land or housing loans originally intended for their dead husbands. There was a measure of assistance, too, for the education of their children. Finally, widows, like the returned nurses and servicemen, often received preferential employment — indeed, in 1930 the Federated Clerks Union noted that able single women were being dismissed from their positions in order to find employment for war widows. One must remember though, that these were monetary measures. They could never compensate for the trial of raising children without fathers or the lonely desperation that was the lot of most widowed women.

The war had momentarily broadened the horizons of most working women. Young and single women entered the clerical and banking professions on an unprecedented scale, wives and daughters sometimes assumed management of businesses and properties in the absence of their menfolk. But the men returned and with them a more conventional division of labour. Not that working women quite lost everything. Despite the officially stated preference to employ only returned servicemen, many employers proved unwilling to part with skilled and reliable workers. A moody or disabled employee was a risky proposition for even the most patriotic businessman. Moreover, for the large number of women widowed or otherwise left single by the war, the option of pursuing a career in preference to marriage became more viable. 'Respectable' single women (those who had lost their husband or fiancé in the war) could choose a new career path as an alternative to dependency and marriage.

Unpaid workers did not fare quite so well in the war's aftermath. The end of hostilities signalled the end of many of the voluntary pursuits that had occupied women throughout the war. Tasks which had once been crucial to the national interest were simply no longer necessary. Women lost not just a sense of self-worth, but also a lively social circle. And they lost their own special claim to patriotism. Throughout the war, men had saluted their sacrifice; women had borne loss and self-denial in a common purpose. But as the men returned home, women found themselves excluded. The RSL became a patriotic elite in Australian society. The only criterion for membership was 'service abroad' but few women could qualify. Nor did the companionship of a man offer a meaningful substitute for the women-centred friendships that were formed in the war years. In fact the men did not make very good companions.

It was not only that so many were hardened and twisted by the experience of war. Having depended so long on their 'mates', men found it impossible to leave them. Rivalling Graham McInnes's memories of those dry-eyed widows at Anzac Day were the men that he observed clustering in the Naval and Military Club in Melbourne. It was not the beer or the gambling that drew them there but rather 'the Anzac dream' — a dream known only to a select circle of men:

Each man had in his hand either a glass or a silver tankard. Their mouths roared open with meaningless ferocity and frightening geniality as they bellowed at each other across their drinks or broke into cannon roars of gusty laughter. They shouted across each other's speech, drowned each other out, listened not at all, kept up the continuous barking and caterwauling while I stood warily in a corner searching for familiar islands in the sea of noise...

I took a secret stock of the seething mass of men. They were all veterans with R.S.S.I.L.A. badges in their lapels, but their talk was of current matters: the race, who to back for the fifth at Flemington, personal gossip, politics, whether the present Prime Minister S.M. Bruce was a smart fellow or just a tailor's dummy, whether Billy Hughes the war-time P.M. would ever make a comeback. But underneath it all lay a lazy sense of camaraderie, of some secret shared in common and which excluded me, not only because I was of another generation, but because I had not been 'over there'; because the names Gallipoli, Gaba Tepe, Mudros, Anzac Cove, the Somme, Passchendaele, the Ancre, Villers-Bretonneux, held for me no common memories softened by time but only the monstrous overtones of fearful shapes looming through the mists of myth and somehow unrelated to the bawling and shouting here in the unfamiliar club. I was on my own island; with the noisy sea of talk but not of it.[7]

Most women, of course, had not been 'over there' either.

Mirroring the social exclusion of women was their political disenfranchisement. The conscription debate had divided Australian society but, whichever side they took, women had one

1913

1914 — 1918

1919

Figure 7.5

Evolution of a digger
(*Aussie*, no. 12, 1919)

■ What is the message
in Lance Mattinson's
cartoon?

thing in common: by supporting the 'pros' or the 'antis', they made a political decision — they exercised their citizenship. Indeed, as we have seen, women were central to the debate; 'the mother's vote' was crucial. Politics after the war no longer depended on women's participation. Their interests and the national interest seemed, once again, to be altogether different. Men resumed control of the political agenda and the political process.

At a more subtle level, women were increasingly marginalised from the major strands of Australian culture as a result of the war. The evolution of the Anzac digger as the symbol of Australia meant that now nationhood was equated with masculinity. Women — who could at best be only *mothers* of Anzacs — were excluded from the new definition of Australian identity.

Of all the women studied in this book, it was women of non-British descent who were the greatest losers in the post-war years. After the war, many 'alien' husbands and sons were deported; those who returned to their Australian communities carried with them the stigma of their internment. Australia had never been a particularly tolerant or cosmopolitan society. The hatred necessary to prosecute the war had not just marginalised an entire section of the population; it had diminished all Australians. And it should be remembered that European families were not the only casualties of this quest to achieve a loyal 'British' society. In the 1930s, Aboriginal people continued their long struggle for citizenship rights, appealing to the government to grant them a vote in what was, after all, their country. But the war had hardened Australians to such entreaties: if nothing else, Australia was a white man's country. Another war, another generation, would pass before Aboriginal people gained even the most basic rights of citizenship.

Ultimately, the quest for racial purity harmed even those it was intended to protect. The war gave rise to a pro-natalist (pro-birth) movement of unprecedented scale. With the population decimated by war, women were told to raise a new battalion of babies and populate the empty, undefended spaces of Australia. In the decade after the war, more women died in childbirth than all the soldiers who had been killed at Gallipoli. No one has raised any monuments to them.

Figure 7.6

Memorial plaque issued to the family of George Smallholme, killed in the Great War (bronze, 12 cm diameter)
(Photograph courtesy the Fleming family, Merimbula, New South Wales)

■ Plaques like this one were issued to the next of kin of all the Empire's 'fallen'. What comfort would such a gesture have brought to the bereaved?

■ Who is the female figure in the centre?

The Great War had been heralded as the war to end all wars. It wasn't. As the Armistice drew near, a columnist in the *Woman Voter* predicted that a purely military victory would settle nothing. If no attempt was made to change the causes of war, the armies would march again.

Suggestions for study

To discuss

1 Why do you think an Australian woman, visiting the Australian war cemetery at Villers-Bretonneux in 1994, wrote 'Vive La Republic' in the visitors book?

2 What effect do you think the Great War had on Australians' attitudes to women of non-British background?

To write about

1 The year is 1930. You are the wife of a soldier settler facing eviction from your wheat farm because you cannot meet the minimum repayments. Put a case to the authorities against your eviction. Note that your husband's health has been affected by the war and that your four children are all under the age of ten.

2 You are a former Army nursing sister who has returned to her parents' home after four years of service overseas. Write a letter to one of your fellow Army nurses discussing the process of readjusting to civilian life.

3 Draw up a 'balance sheet' showing the short- and long-term effects of the war on the status of women in Australia.

To research

1 Using a street directory, identify any place names commemorating battles or famous individuals from the Great War. Are any of the individuals women?

2 What form does the Anzac Day commemoration take at your school? How has the commemoration changed over time? You might be able to consult old issues of your school magazine, or interview former school students or teachers.

3 Find out what happened to Jeanne and her husband in Betty Roland's play, *The Touch of Silk*.

NOTES

Chapter 2

1   Evelyn Davies, letter to her mother from London, 15 July 1915, Evelyn Davies Papers, 3DRL 3398, Australian War Memorial.
2   Davies, letter to her mother, 22 March 1916, *ibid.*
3   Davies, undated letter to her mother from Cairo, *ibid.*
4   Diary of Sister Elsie Cook, 19 September 1918, PR 82/135, Australian War Memorial.
5   Diary of Sister Elsie Tranter, 14 December 1916; 10 January 1917, 3DRL 4081, Australian War Memorial.
6   *ibid.* 3 February 1917.
7   *ibid.* 6 February 1917.
8   Diary of Alice Kitchen, Ms 9627, La Trobe Library.
9   Tranter Diary, 29 January 1917.
10 Diary of Sister Lydia King, 3DRL 6040, Australian War Memorial.
11 Kitchen Diary, 9–11 August 1915.
12 Cook Diary, 30 April, 1 May 1915.
13 Kitchen Diary, 10 July 1915.
14 King Diary, 28 April 1915.
15 Matron Wilson, letter to her sister Minnie from Mudros Bay, Lemnos, 6 August 1915, 3DRL 7819, Australian War Memorial.
16 Diary of Sister D.D. Richmond, 11 August 1915, 2DRL 783, Australian War Memorial.
17 Cook Diary, 12–24 June 1917.
18 King Diary, 1 September 1915.
19 Cook Diary, 6–12 December 1916.
20 Tranter Diary, 27 February 1917.
21 Davies, letter to her mother, 22 April 1917, 3DRL 3398B, Folder 3, Australian War Memorial.
22 Tranter Diary, 28 June 1917.
23 *ibid.* 1 September 1917.
24 *ibid.* 3 April 1917.
25 Cited in Patsy Adam Smith, *Australian Women at War*, Nelson, Melbourne, 1986, p. 32.
26 Tranter Diary, 22 March 1918.
27 *ibid.* 28 March – 9 April 1918.
28 Cook Diary, 30 May – 1 June 1918.
29 *ibid.* 16 July 1918.
30 Tranter Diary, 2 May 1917.
31 *ibid.* 19 June 1917.
32 *ibid.* 3 April 1917.
33 *ibid.* 14 April 1918.
34 *ibid.* 1 April 1918.
35 Diary of Sister Hilda Loxton, 4 May 1916, 2DRL 1172, Australian War Memorial.
36 Tranter Diary, 28 April 1918.
37 Davies, letter to her mother, 12 November 1916, 3DRL 3398, Australian War Memorial.
38 Tranter Diary, 5 May 1917.
39 Diary of Sister Laura Grubb, Thursday [1917], PR 83/40, Australian War Memorial.
40 *ibid.* Wednesday, 29 [August 1917].
41 *ibid.*
42 *ibid.* Monday, 3 [September 1917].
43 Cited in J. Bassett, *Guns and Brooches: Australian Army Nursing from the Boer War to the Gulf War*, Oxford University Press, Melbourne, 1992, p. 79.
44 *ibid.*
45 Tranter Diary, 10 April 1918.
46 Richmond Diary, 27 September 1918.
47 Tranter Diary, 11 November 1918.
48 Loxton Diary, 30 November 1918.
49 *ibid.* 10 January 1919.

Chapter 3

1   Evidence of Jessie Moira Barnett to Industrial Commission of New South Wales, Bank Officers' State Conciliation Committee, 1928, Noel Butlin Archives of Business and Labour, Canberra, A2/3716, pp. 1–5.
2   *Woman Voter*, 6 April 1916. This weekly publication was produced by the Women's Political Association in Melbourne.
3   Cited in Jan Bassett, 'Lyla Barnard: Khaki Girl', in Marilyn Lake and Farley Kelly (eds), *Double Time: Women in Victoria 150 Years*, Penguin, Ringwood, 1985, p. 271.
4   *ibid.*
5   *Argus*, 3 August 1917, p. 8, cited in Bassett, 'Lyla Barnard', p. 270.
6   *Woman Voter*, 6 April 1916.

7   *Soldier*, 5 January 1917.

8   AIF Despatches, cited in 'Women War Workers', Jensen Papers, Accession No. MP 598/30, Dept of Supply, Item 15, Australian Archives Victoria.

9   Michael McKernan, *The Australian People and the Great War*, Nelson, Sydney 1984, pp. 66–7.

10 *Red Cross Record*, January 1917.

11 Red Cross Society, *The Red Cross and Belgium Fête Book*, Adelaide 1915, p. 9.

12 *Red Cross Record*, January 1917.

13 *Soldier*, 4 August 1916.

14 *Red Cross Record*, June 1917.

15 *ibid.*

16 Frederick J. ⸻s, *Cheer Up: A Story of War Work*, Cheer ⸻ Society Incorporated, Adelaide 1920, pp. 24–5.

17 *Red Cross Record*, July 1916.

18 *Argus*, 28 July 1917, p. 8, cited in Bassett, 'Lyla Barnard', p. 271.

19 Mills, *Cheer Up*, pp. 24–5.

20 *ibid.* pp. 60–1.

21 *ibid.* pp. 58–9.

22 *ibid.* pp. 71, 154.

23 *ibid.* p 107.

24 *Soldier*, 30 March 1917.

25 *ibid.* 29 September 1916.

26 *ibid.* 8 September 1916.

27 *ibid.* 11 August 1916.

28 McKernan, *Australian People and the Great War*, p. 70.

29 *Red Cross Record*, October 1917.

Chapter 4

1   Quoted in Pam Young, *Proud to be a Rebel: The Life and Times of Emma Miller*, University of Queensland Press, St Lucia, 1991, p. 212.

2   Cited in Malcolm Saunders, 'Women fighting for peace: Charles Strong and the Women's International League for Peace and Freedom', *Victorian Historical Journal*, vol. 64, no. 1, April 1993, p. 17.

3   *Socialist*, 12 May 1916, p. 2, cited in Joy Damousi, 'Socialist women and gendered space: the anti-conscription and anti-war campaigns of 1914–18', *Labour History*, no. 60, May 1991, p. 11.

4   *Woman Voter*, 30 March 1916, p. 2.

5   *Daily Standard*, 10 July 1917, cited in Raymond Evans, '"All the passion of our womanhood": Margaret Thorp and the Battle of the Brisbane School of Arts', in Joy Damousi & Marilyn Lake (eds), *Gender and War: Australians at War in the Twentieth Century*, Cambridge University Press, Melbourne, 1995, p. 240.

6   Cited in Evans, 'All the passion of our womanhood', p. 248.

7   *Daily Standard*, 10 July 1917.

8   'The Call to Arms', anon., *High School Chronicle*, Sydney Girls High School, September 1917.

9   *Special Appeal by Women to Women: Manifesto*, Australian Women's Peace Army, Merrifield Collection, La Trobe Library, Ms 13045.

10 *Bi-Weekly No!*, 28 November 1917.

11 *Australian Worker*, Conscription Supplement, 19 October 1916.

12 *Mirror*, 29 October 1916, p. 4.

13 *Sydney Mail*, 15 August 1917, cited in Lucy Taksa, '"Defence not Defiance [sic]": Social Protest and the NSW General Strike of 1917', *Labour History*, no. 60, May 1991, p. 21.

14 Quoted in Judith Smart, 'Feminists, food and the fair price: the cost of living demonstrations in Melbourne, August–September 1917', *Labour History*, no. 50, May 1986, pp. 119–20. Subsequent references to these riots are also drawn from Smart's excellent account.

15 *ibid.*

16 *ibid.* p. 117.

Chapter 5

1   Lyall Family Papers, Ms 10132, La Trobe Library, Victoria.

2   *ibid.*

3   Editorial, *Red Cross Record*, June 1917.

4   Patsy Adam Smith, *Australian Women at War*, Nelson, Melbourne, 1986, pp. 73–4, quoting her grandmother.

5   *National Leader*, 19 January 1917, cited in Carmel Shute, 'Heroines and heroes: sexual mythology in Australia, 1914–1918', *Hecate*, vol. 1, no. 1. January 1975, p. 12.

6   *ibid.* 1 January 1917.

7   Kathleen Chute-Erson, 'Killed in Action', *Red Cross Record*, March 1920.

8   Mary Gilmore, 'These Fellowing Men', *The Passionate Heart*, Angus & Robertson, Sydney, 1918.

9   Mary Gilmore, 'The Mother', reproduced in W.H. Wilde, *Courage a Grace: A Biography of Dame Mary Gilmore*, Melbourne University Press, Melbourne, 1988, pp.192–3.

10 'Roll of Honour', *Sydney Morning Herald*, 25 April 1916.

11 'On Active Service', *ibid*, 12 July 1919.

12 'The King Unveils Memorial', *Argus*, 23 July 1938.

13 *Queenslander*, 1 January 1916.

14   *The American Magazine of Art* (1919), cited in K.S. Inglis, 'Men, women and war memorials', *Daedalus*, Fall 1987, vol. 116, no. 4, p. 51.

15   Graham McInnes, *The Road to Gundagai*, Hamish Hamilton, London, 1965, pp. 282–3.

16   Cited in Dennis Jeans, 'The Anzac Memorial, Sydney: towards a secular culture' in *Australians 1938: A Bicentennial Bulletin*, no. 4, November 1981, p. 50.

17   *Sun*, 18 July 1932.

18   *The Book of the Anzac Memorial, New South Wales*, Sydney 1934, pp. 47–50.

19   'Noble Clay', *Sun*, 25 May 1932.

20   *Sun*, 7 July 1932.

21   'Nude Woman on Anzac Cross', *ibid*, 14 July 1932.

Chapter 6

1   D.A. Walsh, 'The Enemy in Our Midst: Venereal Diseases', *Proceedings of the University of Sydney Society for Combating Venereal Diseases*, 1916–17.

2   *Woman Voter*, 18 May 1916, p. 3.

3   *ibid*.

4   Address of Vida Goldstein to Women's Convention on the Social Evil, reported in *Woman Voter*, 18 May 1916, p. 2.

5   *West Australian Parliamentary Debates*, vol. 57, p. 1255.

6   *Woman Voter*, 11 May 1916.

7   *ibid*. 18 May 1916.

8   *ibid*. 29 June 1916.

9   *ibid*.

10   *ibid*. 18 May 1916.

11   Cited in Julie Tisdale, '"The Future Mothers of Our Race": Venereal Disease and the Amateur in Melbourne During World War I', unpublished BA Honours thesis, History, Monash University, 1994, pp. 40–1.

12   Scott, *Official History of Australia in the War*, p. 105.

13   *ibid*. p. 139.

14   Letter from Daisy Schoeffel to Hon. H. Gregory, Australian Archives (ACT), CRS 457, Item 406/1.

15   Cited in Gerhard Fischer, *Enemy Aliens: Internment and the Homefront Experience in Australia, 1914-1920*, University of Queensland Press, St Lucia, 1929, pp. 128–9.

16   *ibid*. p. 270.

17   *ibid*.

Chapter 7

1   'Heartless treatment of soldiers' widows', *Diggers' Gazette*, 15 November 1919, p. 11.

2   George Johnston, *My Brother Jack*, Fontana, Melbourne, 1987, pp. 6–7.

3   *Soldier*, 19 January 1917.

4   *ibid*. 17 January 1917.

5   Cited in Patsy Adam Smith, *Australian Women at War*, Nelson, Melbourne, 1984, pp. 107–8.

6   Cited in Marilyn Lake, *The Limits of Hope: Soldier Settlement in Victoria*, Oxford University Press, Melbourne, 1987, p. 169.

7   Graham McInnes, *The Road to Gundagai*, Hamish Hamilton, London, 1965, pp. 231–2.

INDEX

SOURCES

Sources and details for all documents and figures are cited on the page where the material appears. They are reproduced with kind permission of the copyright holders. Also acknowledged are copyright holders as follows:

Cover
Front cover illustration based on: 'Women with AIF reinforcements [Sydney]' c. 1915, photograph courtesy of the Australian War Memorial, H11568
Back cover photograph: 'Winged Victory', Marrickville War Memorial, erected 1919, photograph courtesy Alex Scates Frances.

Documents
2.1, 2.2 & 2.11 3DRL 3398, 3398B, AWM; **2.3, 2.4 2.6 & 2.13** DRL 4081, 3DRL 4081, AWM; **2.5** 2DRL 783, AWM; **2.7, 2.8 & 2.12** PR 83/40 (6), AWM; **2.9** 57/1, AWM; **2.10** PR 82/40, AWM; **3.8** Mary Gilmore: 'An Australian Gum Leaf', reproduced with permission of the Public Trustee and ETT Imprint; **3.9** *A Fortunate Life* by A.B. Facey, Penguin Books Australia Ltd; **4.1** La Trobe Library, Melbourne; **4.2** Ms 13045, Merrifield Collection, La Trobe Library, Melbourne; **4.3** La Trobe Library, Melbourne; **4.7** Ms 2123, La Trobe Library, Melbourne; **4.8** Ms 3637, La Trobe Library, Melbourne; **4.10, 4.11, 4.12, 4.13 & 4.15** Ms 3200, La Trobe Library, Melbourne; **4.14** Copyright Jane Glad; **4.16, 4.17 & 4.18** Ms 13045, La Trobe Library, Melbourne; **5.1** Ms 10145, La Trobe Library, Melbourne; **5.2** Ms 12598, La Trobe Library, Melbourne; **5.5** Ms 12598, La Trobe Library, Melbourne; **5.6** La Trobe Library, Melbourne; **5.7** Ms 12598, Hope Papers, La Trobe Library, Melbourne; **6.2** 'A Young Prisoner of War' from *The Home Fires* by Anthony Splivalo, Fremantle Arts Centre Press; **7.1** Mitchell Library, State Library of New South Wales; **7.2** *A Fence Around the Cuckoo* by Ruth Park, Penguin Books Australia Ltd; **7.3** By permission of Currency Press, Sydney. First Published by Currency Press, 1988; **7.4** Ms 9627, La Trobe Library, Melbourne.

Figures
1.1 Government Printing Office Collection, State Library of New South Wales; **2.1** La Trobe Newspaper Collection, State Library of Victoria; **2.2** AO5410, AWM; **2.3** JO1748, AWM; **2.4** P1360/02/01, AWM; **2.5** JO1714, AWM; **2.6** PO156/81/43, AWM; **2.7** PO1790.001, AWM; **2.8** 2DRL/1172, AWM; **2.9** Ms 3637, National Library of Australia; **2.10** PO156/81/66, AWM; **2.11** HO9726, AWM; **2.12** PO 1790.002, AWM; **2.13** CO4337, AWM; **2.14** JO5885, AWM; **2.15** AO1178, AWM; **2.16** PO 190 032, AWM; **3.1** La Trobe Newspaper Collection, State Library of Victoria; **3.2** HO2334, AWM; **3.3** H11568, AWM; **3.4** HO2438, AWM; **3.5** H11579, AWM; **3.6** Ms 12004, Lucy Family Papers, La Trobe Library, Melbourne; **3.7** AO5371, AWM; **3.8** La Trobe Newspaper Collection, State Library of Victoria; **3.9** H16130, AWM; **3.12** Ms 10332, La Trobe Library, Melbourne; **4.1** Merrifield Collection, La Trobe Library, Melbourne; **5.1** Used by permission of A.P. Watt Ltd on behalf of The National Trust; **5.3** Ms 3637, Ferguson Papers, National Library of Australia; **6.2** La Trobe Newspaper Collection, State Library of Victoria; **6.4** PO595/174/156, AWM; **7.1** P1425/17, AWM; **7.3** P1102/40/21, AWM; **7.4** P1432/04, AWM.

All quotations within the general text are referenced and their sources and details cited in the notes on pages 158 to 160. Quotations are reproduced with kind permission of the copyright holders. Also acknowledged are copyright holders as follows:

Quoted matter
p.1 'War is Women's...', La Trobe Library, Melbourne; **p.6** 'do their bit', **p.13** 'On entering the...', **p.16** '12.6.17: Boating on...', **p.17** '6.12.16: Great excitement...', **p.22** '30.5.18: All the...', from Lt. Col. Peter Cook (RL); **p.83** 'As the Mothers...', Ms 13045, **p.100** 'I sent my...', Ms 10132, **p.103** 'you would value...', Ms 10132, La Trobe Library, Melbourne; **p.103–4** 'Some women wouldn't...', Penguin Books Australia Ltd; **p.107** 'Dead are the...', **p.109** 'Out in the...', reproduced with permission of the Public Trustee and ETT Imprint; **p.124** 'Cairo will do...', 'diseased soldiers are...', 'The war has...', **p.125** 'Every seat along...', 'The girl's point...', 'education, kind treatment...', **p.125–6** 'the path of...', **p.126** 'A young soldier...', La Trobe Library, Melbourne.